Nigel Mansell

A photographic portrait

First published in June 2007

A catalogue record for this book is available from
the British Library

ISBN 9 781 84425 631 0

Library of Congress control no 2007922003

Published by Haynes Publishing,
Sparkford, Yeovil, Somerset BA22 7JJ, England
Tel: 01963 442030 Fax: 01963 440001
Int. tel: +44 1963 442030 Int. fax: +44 1963 440001
E-mail: sales@haynes.co.uk
Website: www.haynes.co.uk

Haynes North America Inc.
861 Lawrence Drive, Newbury Park,
California 91320, USA

All pictures in this book are courtesy of LAT Photographic.

The publisher wishes to thank all at LAT for their collaboration on
this book, and in particular Peter Higham, Kathy Ager, Tim Wright,
Kevin Wood, Stephen Carpenter, Matt Smith and Emma Champion.

Design and layout by Richard Parsons

Printed and bound in Great Britain by
J. H. Haynes & Co. Ltd

CONTENTS PAGE The closest that Nigel Mansell got to winning at
Monaco was in the 1992 race, which he led from the start until deciding
to make an unscheduled tyre change with half a dozen laps to go.
Ayrton Senna snatched the lead – and nothing that Nigel was able to do
on fresh rubber would dislodge the Brazilian's McLaren-Honda.

Nigel Mansell
A photographic portrait

Photographs by **LAT** • Words by **Mike Doodson**

CONTENTS

Even though it's 12 years (at the time of writing) since Nigel Mansell drove his last F1 race, his achievements still resonate with the British public. Here was someone with whom any working man could identify. A factory worker who had once washed windows to help fund his racing activities, he endured privation, pain and indignity in a search for the ultimate success which he and his wife Rosanne never doubted would one day be theirs.

Having acquired a distaste for most journalists at an early stage of his career, Nigel was at his best behind the wheel. While he didn't enjoy extensive testing, he worked well with engineers and his race performances were enviably consistent. There was no type of circuit which he disliked and he usually behaved correctly, though never gently, with rival drivers. If he was sometimes a little hard on machinery, that was because he was working it to the maximum.

By strength of character, sheer stubbornness and a sometimes irrational refusal to accept that anyone but he was right, Nigel Mansell went from indebtedness in a suburb of Birmingham to a palatial mansion in Florida, then to owning his own golf resort in Devon. Adored by fans who physically broke down barriers during a British GP to be closer to him, he claimed that putting on a good show for them was more important than money. He won 31 GPs in an F1 career that spanned 15 years. He won only one world championship, in 1992, but he's still in demand. He has yet to announce a full retirement from motor racing and his appearances behind the wheel, though increasingly rare, are guaranteed to pull in a crowd.

On leaving school, during the daytime he worked alongside his father, Eric, as an apprentice engineer with Lucas Aerospace in Birmingham. At night he would go out washing windows to find a few more pounds for his karting career. He was only 18 years old when he married his wife Rosanne, who shared all his early hardships with him. They went without new clothes and holidays to support his racing. For several years Rosanne was the family breadwinner, working as a demonstrator with the West Midlands Gas Board when Nigel was still struggling in the lower echelons of British club racing.

At Brands Hatch in 1978 he had somersaulted off the road in a Formula Ford car and almost lost his life. That, as Nigel told me in 1986, was as low as it ever got. "I'd raised a lot of finance by selling the house and many of our possessions. I'd had a very good job at Lucas Aerospace and they'd said that I had to decide between them and racing for my career, so I'd told myself that you're only young once and I'd go for racing. If it goes wrong, I thought, perhaps I'd go back to engineering.

"It was only three weeks after I'd handed in my notice that I had the accident at Brands Hatch in which I broke my neck. I was told categorically that I was very lucky not to be a quadriplegic, categorically that I would never race again. I was lying in hospital all on my own, no friends and no relatives close by to visit. I had no job and no income: I was only getting paid for when I was driving, because I had a sponsored drive that was paying me, I think, £100 per race. That was the only income I had coming in except for what my wife was earning, and she couldn't come and see me during the week, because she was working to earn the

money to pay the rent. That was, for sure, the lowest ebb of my career and my life. I thought I had screwed up everything. Not to put too fine a point on it, I'd buggered up our whole life. It was really bad."

Nigel's fierce devotion to Rosanne and their three children made him different from many other drivers. He has always stood out as a monogamous hero whose love life is far too boring for the gossip columns. "She's the most amazing woman I know," he said of Rosanne in 1986, and their partnership has endured. "I go through periods when I miss her so much, and there are other times when she's a bundle of surprises, even to me, her husband. I love her so much. The support and the energy and the vigour and the dimension of her attitude have been undiminished, all through our relationship. She has so much faith in me that there's no way I would have got where I am without my dear wife Rosanne. She is so special that, well, I suppose there should be a statue erected to commemorate what she has done for me."

His feelings towards some of the people he has encountered in F1 are considerably less affectionate. On the way to the top, he has rubbed up some of them the wrong way. Nobody could ever be equivocal about Nigel Mansell. To those who shared unwaveringly in his towering self-belief, he remained a good friend. All others were dismissed as worthless non-believers.

It took a long time to go from backmarker to front-runner. Not for Nigel the structured career, the planned ascent or the compliant sponsor. He had to battle hard at every stage, sometimes being forced to accept setbacks which would have stranded anyone else. He would certainly not have succeeded without the financial and moral support of people like businessman Alan McKechnie or journalist Peter Windsor. The final step up into F1, in the late summer of 1980, came thanks to Lotus boss Colin Chapman, who happened to be looking for a promising British driver at that time. It became a close relationship – and Chapman's sudden death in December 1982 left Nigel with precious few friends inside the team.

The lowest point of the years with Lotus was a heart-breaking afternoon at Monaco in 1984, when he took the lead under appalling conditions, only to spin off the road and crash out of contention. In a famous TV interview with Murray Walker, he put up the excuse that he'd hit a patch of white paint on the road, but the truth lay somewhat deeper. That morning he'd had

to listen to yet another put-down from his own team manager, and he was depressed and angry when the race started. And he'd made a most unprofessional mistake by trying to extend his lead over the McLaren of Alain Prost instead of holding the gap constant.

"In the five years I was at Lotus, we only won one race," he would observe, "and that tells the whole story in itself." He needed some powerful motivation to keep him going through those difficult years, and not for the first time he fell back on his own faith in himself. It's a faith that he demonstrated long before his Grand Prix days, through years without any form of sponsorship and through anxious weeks spent in hospital with injuries that would have stopped a lesser man.

Even when his grit and determination earned him a contract to drive Frank Williams' increasingly competitive Honda-powered car in 1985, he was still not regarded as a front-runner. Frank had already recruited Nelson Piquet to lead the Williams-Honda team in 1986. Piquet was the obvious star, having already won two titles at Brabham, and he was able to command what was then a record salary. Only when Nigel made his breakthrough with two accomplished and aggressive victories at the end of 1985 were the sport's opinion-makers forced to recognise that he was a far better driver than most of them had ever imagined.

His physical fitness was already legend: he has always had a fully equipped gymnasium at home, not to mention the firmest handshake in the paddock. Why, then, did he have to be supported on the podium after winning the British GP at Brands Hatch in 1986? "Oh, that was because I was driving the team's spare car, which had been set up for Nelson Piquet and not for me," he explains. "I made the mistake of not checking the seat belts before I got into it, and the buckle was right up in my solar plexus. I couldn't breathe properly throughout that race.

"It was also a truly emotional event for me: the elation of winning my home Grand Prix only hit me after I'd won, but when it did I sort of deflated myself in

OPPOSITE The Lotus period of Nigel's career began when he was picked out at a test by team owner Colin Chapman. The relationship flourished until Chapman's sudden death in 1982, when Nigel found himself at odds with F1 manager Peter Warr.

Nigel on Rosanne: "She's the most amazing woman I know... She has so much faith in me that there's no way I would have got where I am without my dear wife Rosanne. She is so special that, well, I suppose there should be a statue erected to commemorate what she has done for me."

Nigel on Williams: "When I joined the Williams team, I told Frank that I wanted to be judged, not from the past, not from what people say behind your back to rubbish you – and unfortunately there's too much of that in motor racing – but from my testing with the team, from my racing..."

less than a minute." The crowd responded with equal emotion, but recently introduced FISA rules forbade victory laps because of a fuel limitation (the weight of the fuel expended on the extra lap might put the car below the limit). Nigel overcame that nicely by literally hijacking the Range Rover which was supposed to take him to the medical centre to check his exhausted condition. So Nigel, in effect, forced the driver to do a lap of honour. Nobody at Brands will ever forget that heart-warming gesture.

The victories of 1985 and 1986 were all the sweeter considering the lack of results in his first five years at Lotus. "There's no question that when you win a race, people tend to forget your past achievements," he says. "I was a champion in Formula Ford back in 1977 and won 32 races out of 42, but people only look at your Grand Prix career. The important thing was that once I had done it, I knew how I'd done it. To a certain extent, it is a question of confidence, but also it's a question of knowing where to divert all your energies to get the best result. Before, in past years, I can say that I diverted a lot of energies, certainly in the wrong place. But now I'm a lot wiser: those energies are being channelled much more efficiently with this team than they were at Lotus over the past couple of years."

Much of the credit for the 'new' Mansell and his success was attributable to Frank Williams himself. Though confined to a wheelchair following a road accident in France at the beginning of 1986, Williams had the same passion for physical fitness which Mansell has always had. But there were other common factors. Both have backgrounds in the English provinces, far away from the glamour of London. They share an innate faith in their own abilities. They're both family men whose wives have played an important role in their lives when they needed it most. And Frank has never forgotten the years that he spent in the wilderness, waiting – as Nigel would do – for the opportunity to show the world that determination can vanquish a reputation for hard luck.

"When I joined the Williams team, I told Frank that I wanted to be judged, not from the past, not from what people say behind your back to rubbish you – and unfortunately there's too much of that in motor racing – but from my testing with the team, from my racing and from my approach. I wanted him to be totally fair, and vice versa."

Why, then, did so many sober-minded folk in F1 harbour such negative impressions of Nigel? Perhaps the greatest contributing factor was his awkwardness outside the cockpit. There were times when he seemed to forget that sportsmen are judged not on their social background but on their achievements, making him feel patronised. He was comfortable only when he had people, bought and paid for, around him. For a while it was the California Highway Patrol officer who had stopped him for speeding near Long Beach, and who was subsequently hired as a minder.

There was also a succession of personal managers, none of whom lasted very long. His most enduring management relationship was with Sheridan Thynne, a one-time club-racer who had made friends many years earlier with Frank Williams. Some observers found it significant that Thynne, who came from an aristocratic family which could trace its roots back to the Norman conquest, possessed all of the social graces which Nigel imagined were missing from his own background.

It was typical of the Mansell character that when he moved his family to the Isle of Man (low tax, no tricky foreigners), he built his house on a cliff top, overlooking the Irish Sea but also subject to the gales which blew off it. When his neighbours down the hill politely declined to share in the cost of resurfacing the scruffy public access road which had served them well for years, Nigel decided to build his own private road.

From the moment when he got into F1, Nigel deeply resented his not being taken seriously by everyone. Success with Williams, and his close battle with Piquet and McLaren driver Alain Prost for the 1986 title, should have killed that resentment. But no sooner had the 1988 season started than he discovered what should have been obvious at the end of 1987, that the loss of Honda engines and the move to non-turbo customer Judd V8s, would destroy the team's front-running position. He could have escaped his contract with Williams at the end of that 1987 season, and a driver with more political savvy than Nigel would have done just that.

It was therefore a big relief to him when the call came from Ferrari (not the other way round) to join up in 1989, and he found the Scuderia's blandishments impossible to resist.

The Mansell career blossomed at Ferrari. The Scuderia had not won a championship since 1979, and was going through one of the long dry periods which, at least until the arrival of Michael Schumacher, have marked its history. Although there had been a number of designers and senior engineers from other countries at the factory, it was still a very Italian team, and Italian was the only language spoken. Nigel signed up for an expensive 'deep immersion' course to learn the language, ten hours a day, six days a week. As he ruefully admitted, at the end of it he still couldn't hold a conversation in Italian. "To make things worse, for a week or two I couldn't understand my children and they couldn't understand me."

Winning his first race with Ferrari in 1989 – with a car that hadn't been capable of running trouble-free for more than 100 miles in pre-season testing – set church bells ringing in Maranello and earned him the undying affection of Italian fans. The Ferraris he drove always fell short of the standards of reliability which have since become essential, leaving him with just three wins to show for his two years at Maranello. Nevertheless, he always gave his best at Ferrari and his period there was happy until quite near the end.

The man who ultimately forced Nigel to unpick his links with Italy was the Frenchman Alain Prost, who arrived in 1990 from McLaren, where he had become involved in stern confrontations with Ayrton Senna. Those skills in politics and language which Nigel lacked were meat and drink to Prost, who lost no time in making himself comfortable in the Latin environment. Such situations have always been commonplace at Ferrari – indeed Enzo Ferrari encouraged and exploited them throughout his long life in racing. However, an indignant Mansell, protesting that his position was being undermined, petulantly announced at Silverstone in 1990 that he intended to retire.

Perhaps seeking to divert attention away from what amounted to a psychological defeat, Nigel added that his decision had been spurred by a realisation that he should 'put the family first'. Not even Fleet Street argues when a tough sportsman decides that his family needs him more than his fans do. But many of those who had been present when Nigel made his announcement sensed that the decision might not be written in stone.

Sure enough, when Williams pursued him with an offer for 1991, he did indeed change his mind. Rosanne responded splendidly. "It is always a joint decision," she said. "We are very much a team. It is a decision we both make together. We have been together for so many years, we think the same. But ultimately it will be Nigel's decision whether he will drive next year."

Nigel, meanwhile, had learned that it's always a mistake to make a link between family and career, especially when there are journalists hovering in the hope of getting a headline-grabbing quote. When he returned to F1 for the third and final time, in 1994, no mention was made of what the family's reaction had been to the decision.

Nigel himself always said that he would leave his performances on the race track to speak for him. It was a happy coincidence that throughout his most competitive years in F1 he had an opportunity to measure himself against the very best of the era. Any of those performances will always rank with anything that was achieved by Prost, Senna or Piquet, and there were days when he had all of them beaten squarely.

What was it, then, which made Nigel Mansell such a great driver? Patrick Head, the engineering mastermind behind the successes of the Williams team, said that Nigel didn't waste too much time with his engineers analysing the behaviour of the car. Instead, he brought raw courage to the job of driving.

Speaking in 1992, Head admitted that the team had taken a big gamble in 1991, when they committed themselves to the revolutionary computer-controlled active suspension with which they had been experimenting for almost five years. With a lesser driver than Nigel, the experiment might well have failed horribly.

"With the active suspension the driver doesn't feel understeer or oversteer as he would do with a conventional passive system," explained Head. "That

"To have the motivation to win a world championship you must in turn have those commitments back from the team. When I returned [to Williams] from Ferrari I did so with the belief that I had that motivation and the team had that commitment. I don't think that I was wrong."

means he has to be a bit more courageous to go straight to the limit, and we saw this in the different responses of Nigel and Riccardo Patrese.

"Riccardo is a driver who is very sensitive to 'feel'. I am not saying Nigel isn't, but he very seldom mentions anything about feel or feedback, he just says there's a bit of understeer or whatever. So on his car we can make an adjustment to compensate, like putting on a bit more wing, and – whack! – the time is there.

"It's difficult to say whether one is talking here about talent or just pure, raw speed. Nigel is a very good driver for a team to work with, because he climbs in a car and immediately the time is there, from the first timed lap. He seems to have a very broad acceptance of the behaviour of the car, without affecting his lap time. That makes a team feel good about itself.

"In the race, if the car is not turning into the corners as sharply as he likes, Nigel will just dab the brake pedal and bring the nose down and turn in. With the active suspension we sometimes had problems with aeration of the fluid in the active system, which means that we lost some of the damping characteristic and the car's handling would start to look a bit floppy.

Patrick Head: "It's difficult to say whether one is talking about talent or just pure, raw speed. Nigel is a very good driver for a team to work with, because he climbs in a car and immediately the time is there... That makes a team feel good about itself."

"But it just didn't seem to affect Nigel, whereas with Riccardo if the feedback through the steering wasn't right for him, if it didn't feel perfect – boof! – he would be off the throttle. While Nigel makes his car do what he wants, Riccardo guides the car."

Taking a different perspective on Nigel is Professor Sid Watkins, the internationally renowned neurosurgeon who followed the Grand Prix trail for almost 30 years as the FIA's senior medical officer. The Professor encountered Nigel on a professional basis on several occasions...

"Right from the time when he was first with Lotus, there have been occasions when I could not be sure whether Nigel was pretending, acting or simulating some response for reasons best known to himself," recalls the Professor. "Whenever he appeared to be in trouble, I came to distrust him. There was an interesting event at Dallas in 1984, for example, when I was suddenly called to the finish line, at the end of the race. I was told before I arrived that a driver had collapsed because he had been pushing his car.

"More than 15 years earlier, a rule had been made which banned a driver from pushing his car. When I thought about the driver who was most likely to have forgotten the rule, and who would be pushing his car, it was Nigel who came to my mind. And when I got there, so it proved. There was this heap lying on the floor. Using my foot, I turned it over to make sure who it was. I said, 'you'll be alright, Nigel', then I got back in the safety car and left."

It was not the first time that Nigel had made what appeared to be a miraculous medical recovery. "I remember one of Nigel's first races with Williams, in 1985, when he appeared to have collapsed at the end of the Belgian GP," remembers Professor Watkins. "Even then I had got used to his habits, but this was not a dangerous situation, because the race was over. It was possible that he had collapsed from heat exhaustion, but I knew it was also possible that he was just playing again. So I went down to him and tapped on his helmet. I think he had actually finished fifth , and when he looked up at me, I said, 'Nigel, they want you on the podium.' That revived him immediately and he jumped out of the car and dashed off at great speed up the hill. And when he got to the podium, they would not let him on because he hadn't qualified for it."

Ironically, it was yet another Mansell incident which forced Professor Watkins himself to seek medical attention. "Again, it happened at Spa," he recalls, "at the time when he was racing for Ferrari. There had been an accident at the start in which Nigel's car was hit, and it went into the guardrail. As usual, at the start of the race, I was following in the safety car, a very fast Porsche driven by a former racing driver.

"As we passed, I could see Nigel still in the car, apparently unconscious, with his head down on his arms on the wheel of the car. From previous experience, I wondered, 'Is it real? Or is it not?' By the time we had stopped the Porsche, we had gone round the first corner and a short way down the hill. I got out and ran back up the hill.

"As I did so, I suddenly felt a sharp pain in the calf of my leg. I had snapped a tendon. But I still dashed up round the the corner, to Nigel – who was still lying with his head on his arm. I tapped him on the helmet and

asked him what was wrong. He just looked up and said, 'nothing'. He did not need any medical attention at all. At that point I made a rude remark, turned round and limped back to my car. I had difficulty walking for a few weeks after that, and I still blame Nigel to some extent for my discomfort."

At his peak, in 1992, Nigel was undoubtedly the strongest man in Formula 1 – one look at his neck muscles was proof of that. He talked at Silverstone that year with great enthusiasm about Becketts, the series of left-right-left corners where those neck muscles were tested by the g-forces generated by his Williams FW14B, then (and probably still) the most technically advanced F1 car ever built. It's this extraordinary physical resilience which commanded the admiration from the fans which Mansell treasures. Together with the moustache and the well-muscled body, it represents a tough-guy image which he's happy to promote. But, as Professor Watkins has noted, in fact he's an unusually sensitive person, the very opposite of the public image.

That sensitivity was sorely tested after Nigel's final 'come-back' to F1. In the aftermath of the Imola crash which took Ayrton Senna's life in May 1994, Nigel re-joined Williams for the French GP. His love affair with American racing had ended and he could make himself available back in F1. As Bernie Ecclestone has subsequently revealed, though, the deal very nearly failed to happen.

"Renault asked me to contact Nigel, because when Nigel left Frank in 1992, it wasn't on the best of terms. And I personally thought it [would be] good for Frank, and I think I was proved right, because the team got into gear after he was here, it kicked a few people and it gave Damon [Hill] a lot of confidence. Therefore it was Renault [who wanted it most] and it was good for Frank. I think it was probably good for Formula 1 as well. My contribution actually came about because Mansell was digging in for something, Williams was digging in and there was no way [they looked like agreeing]. So I said, 'OK, I'll pay the difference, to make it happen.' I thought both parties were being stupid."

Hill's championship hopes were obliterated at Adelaide when he was barged off the track by Michael Schumacher, who had just damaged his car's suspension by touching a barrier. With Nigel having shown that he could still win in F1, McLaren-Mercedes boss Ron Dennis offered him a contract for 1995. The

cynics said it would never work, and on this occasion they were right. McLaren's new star couldn't even find room for his derrière in early examples of the chassis, so he missed the first two races of the season.

He was still far from comfortable with the Mk2 version of the McLaren, but this time it was the car's unpredictable handling which was at the root of the problem. It was so bad that in the Spanish GP at Jérez, Nigel did something one never imagined him doing: he abandoned a mechanically healthy racing car. It was the end, finally, of a career which had regularly inspired millions of fans. Nigel Mansell never raced an F1 car again.

Almost three years earlier, less than a month after he had been rewarded with a world title at the 1992 Hungarian GP, Nigel had talked to the press of his struggles as a racing driver in terms – unusual for him – which were both touching and convincing.

"It is very difficult to put into words the sort of commitment you have to make in order to succeed in Formula 1," he reflected. "I am aware of criticisms made of my approach to racing. But I am the way I am because I believe in total sacrifice, a total ability to withstand pain and because I have a total belief in myself and my ability.

"To have the motivation to win a world championship you must in turn have those commitments back from the team. When I returned [to Williams] from Ferrari I did so with the belief that I had that motivation and the team had that commitment. I don't think that I was wrong."

If only he had applied the same criteria to the invitation from McLaren, he might not have been exposed to that final humiliation at Jérez.

Nevertheless, the unhappy memory of that concluding outing in Spain is obliterated by so many glorious, unforgettable moments. And regardless of what the pundits say, Nigel Mansell won the hearts of millions of British fans. They will cherish their memories, at least until another promising Brit comes along to dethrone him.

Professor Sid Watkins: "There have been occasions when I could not be sure whether Nigel was pretending, acting or simulating some response for reasons best known to himself. Whenever he appeared to be in trouble, I came to distrust him."

EARLY YEARS

1976 – 1979

Like almost every driver who has worked his way through to Formula 1, Nigel Mansell started racing in karts, and the first contact he had with the sport came through his father. Eric Mansell bought him his first kart, and the boy won races when the worn-out second-hand equipment lasted. He knew then that he wanted to get to the top, which meant making the expensive move up to cars, and his first encounter with a Formula Ford was at the Mallory Park school in 1975. The young man from Hall Green in Birmingham did seven races with a battered Hawke in 1976, when he was already 22, and he won five of them. By then he was committed to his dream of Formula 1, and the commitment was financial as well as psychological. Amazingly, his new wife Rosanne shared the confidence that he had in himself. In 1978, they sold their flat to pay for five races in a factory March F3 car. He was homeless, jobless and in debt, but he was on his way.

RIGHT At Mallory Park in 1976, at the wheel of a well-worn Formula Ford Hawke. This was his first racing car and he put himself deep in debt to buy it.

The tough days. In 1976 and 1977, Nigel struggled to finance his own Formula Fords (Javelin, top left) or Crosslé (bottom left and top right), until Gloucester businessman Alan McKechnie stepped in and offered some help and a handful of races in his F3 Lola T570 (right). Despite the tight budgets, almost every race in those two years brought a top-three finish and he also received a Commendation in the 1977 Grovewood Awards.

It was at the beginning of 1978 that Nigel and Rosanne sold their flat to fund five races in a works March 783-Toyota. He finished second at Silverstone (in the wet) but struggled against the stronger Ralt competition in the other races. Still, he was being noticed and picked up an offer from the ICI team to race an F2 Chevron at Donington Park (bottom right), though he did not qualify.

The 1979 season brought a breakthrough: a paid-for drive with the Unipart-funded March F3 team. Team boss Dave Price (seated on wheel, top left) was stuck with the sponsor's choice of Triumph Dolomite Sprint engines, which were no match for the rival Toyota units. Still, Nigel used his wet-road ability to pick up one win, at Silverstone (above and left).

By 1980, Nigel's ability had earned him some admirers in the press. Journalist Peter Windsor and photographer David Phipps had seen his exploits in the Unipart F3 car (above left) and had recommended him to Lotus boss Colin Chapman, who in turn mentioned Nigel's name to Ralt's Ron Tauranac. Joining team regular Geoff Lees (above), Nigel crashed in his first F2 race and only managed to finish twice in four outings with the Honda-powered car.

LOTUS

1980 — 1984

In 1978, Nigel had the good fortune to be observed in his F3 March by a perceptive journalist, Peter Windsor. It was through Windsor that Lotus boss Colin Chapman became aware of the newcomer's potential. It was another stroke of luck that Chapman had decided he needed a British driver for his team, and in a test at the Ricard circuit, in 1979, Nigel impressed Chapman enough to get a contract for 1980 which promised him three F1 outings. The three races produced two DNFs and a DNQ, but they did earn Nigel a full year's extension on his contract. When he finished third in the Belgian GP of 1981, only the fifth race of the year, Chapman raised his pay and extended the contract. Nigel's place in F1 had been consolidated and the hard times were behind him. After Chapman's sudden death in December 1982, though, his place inside the team was compromised by some spectacular driving errors.

RIGHT Dallas 1984: a near miss. Having taken his first-ever pole position in qualifying, Nigel was contesting the lead with Keke Rosberg's Williams-Honda in the closing laps. In the almost intolerable Texas heat, the Englishman clipped the wall several times, eventually causing gearbox damage which stopped him short of the line. In an ill-advised attempt to push the car home, Nigel collapsed, unconscious...

Nigel joined the Lotus F1 team in 1980 as a test driver with a contract from his mentor Colin Chapman that promised him three races. The first of them was the Austrian GP at the Österreichring, where he elected to go to the line despite a fuel leak into the cockpit. Driving in agony from petrol burns, he only stopped when the Cosworth engine expired with 13 laps to go. Nigel eventually established a happy relationship with team-mate Elio de Angelis, seen here chatting to Lotus engineer Peter Wright. The lavish Essex sponsorship came courtesy of the mysterious Monaco-based oil trader David Thieme, who subsequently disappeared from F1 when he was arrested in Switzerland.

On only his sixth attempt in an F1 car, Nigel earned a podium place. The occasion was the Belgian GP of 1981, at the cramped Zolder circuit, after a confused race which was stopped at one stage following a start-line incident which fatally injured a mechanic. The race was won by Carlos Reutemann's Williams from Jacques Laffite's Talbot-Ligier.

NEXT PAGE First time out at Monaco, in 1981, Nigel discovered the hard way that the barriers and kerbs don't have any absorbency in them. He retired with suspension damage and gained a particular respect for the most famous street circuit of them all. He was destined never to win the race.

As an innovative engineer, Colin Chapman pioneered many of the features seen on all of today's F1 cars, but his celebrated 'double-chassis' Lotus 88 of 1981 (right) was not destined to be one of them. Repeated arguments with scrutineers and the sport's international federation came to a head at Nigel's first British GP, at Silverstone, where the controversial car was finally thrown out during Friday practice. It was hastily converted overnight into a Lotus 87, but Nigel was unable to qualify. Later, Chapman cut his losses and announced a new deal involving JPS for the remainder of the season in a PR announcement (below) at Brands Hatch.

John Player
John Player Special
ESSEX
TISSOT QUARTZ
12
MICHELIN
MICHELIN
Visit
THEODORE
Car Stripes

Although the 1981 season was to be one of the most turbulent in Lotus history, with controversy over the legality of the 'double-chassis' car and scandal involving sponsor David Thieme, Nigel got some decent results on to the books. He finished third in the Belgian GP at Zolder and took another point here, at Jarama in Spain, for a sixth place.

In the final race of the 1981 season, in Las Vegas (upper left), Nigel fends off former Lotus team-mate Mario Andretti, who was about to end an unrewarding year with Alfa Romeo, while René Arnoux attacks on the inside with his Renault. The only one of the three to earn points was Nigel, in fourth. The following year, at Long Beach (above), Nigel struggled with his under-powered Cosworth V8, but at least he picked up third place in Brazil (lower left), where the cars of Piquet and Rosberg were disqualified.

At Monaco in 1982, though hardly competitive, Nigel gave his best. When the turbo in Pironi's Ferrari expired on the last lap, Nigel found himself in fourth place, a lap behind.

After failing to score at Detroit in 1982 (above), Nigel had an accident on the second lap of the Canadian GP which trapped his hand in the steering wheel and injured his left wrist. He was forced to sit out the Dutch GP while undergoing physiotherapy at home in Birmingham and he arrived at Brands Hatch (right) with a heavy brace on his arm. Despite severe pain, he started the race, only to retire when the car's poor handling got too much for him.

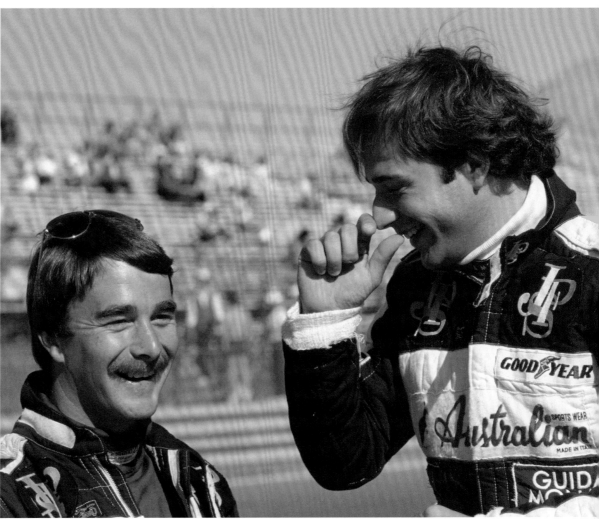

Before his death at the end of 1982, Colin Chapman had negotiated a deal with Renault for the supply of turbo powerplants in 1983. For the first half of the season, however, there were only enough engines for one car, and Renault insisted the privilege went to Elio de Angelis. Nevertheless, still with the old Cosworth non-turbo (left), Nigel plodded on, and there were no hard feelings towards de Angelis (above).

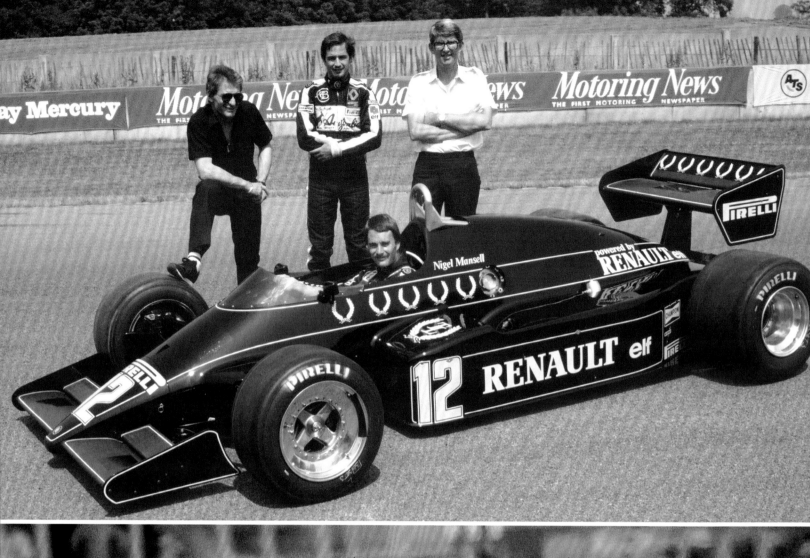

New Lotus boss Peter Warr signed French engineer Gérard Ducarouge (upper left, in black) early in 1983 to design a compact new car around the Renault V6. By superhuman effort, two cars were completed in five weeks and presented at Silverstone. After some electrical dramas with his prized new turbo engine in practice, Nigel took the completely untested Lotus 94T from 18th on the grid to an amazing fourth place in its first ever race. Fellow Brit Derek Warwick (right, in Brazil) was, and remained, a good friend to Nigel. At Hockenheim (lower left), Nigel was forced to use the older Lotus 93T in qualifying, although he raced the newer 94T, until its engine failed after one lap.

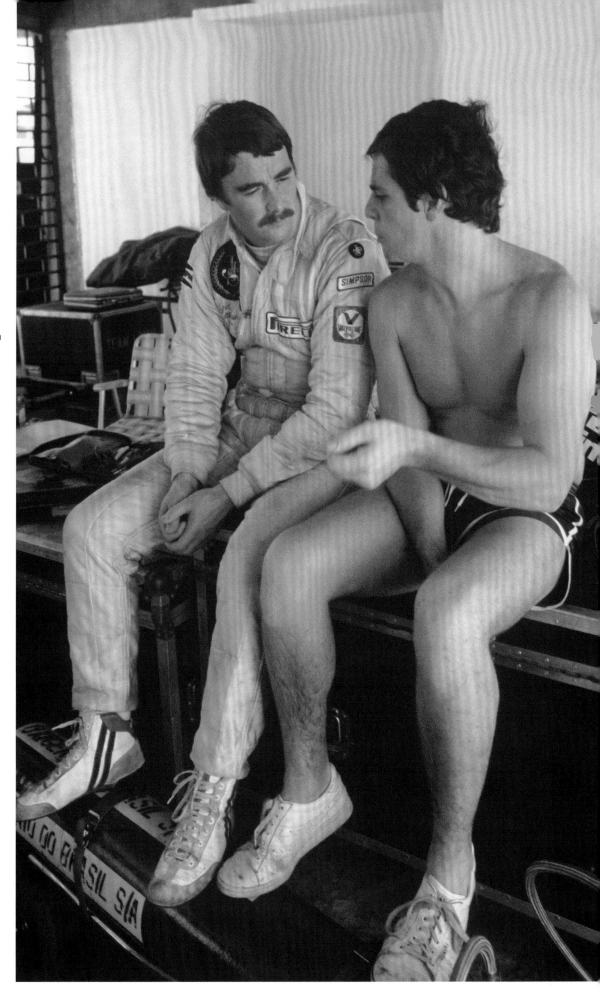

Renault power, together with the impetus provided by Gérard Ducarouge's arrival as chief designer, made for a joyful end to the 1983 season for Nigel and Lotus. In the European GP at Brands Hatch (above) he qualified third and took his first British podium finish (note future multiple champions Piquet and Prost helping to celebrate), and for a while cemented his position at Lotus under Peter Warr, who had not always been a fan. The final GP of the year, in South Africa (upper right), saw an early retirement. Back in the UK (right), Nigel took part in a televised rallysprint event with a factory-backed Rover SD1.

The 1984 season was to be Nigel's last at Lotus, although everything looked fine from the cockpit when the onboard picture (above) was taken during qualifying for round 2 at Kyalami in South Africa. A run of four DNFs in the first four races soured an increasingly flimsy relationship between the driver and team boss Peter Warr, and there were much-publicised incidents at Monaco and Detroit for which Nigel was held responsible. The Lotus 95T was competitive though fragile, but after the fourth round at Imola (right), where he spun out after brake failure, Nigel was able, briefly, to compete with Prost's McLaren in the French GP at Dijon (below), and finished third.

The soaking wet Monaco GP of 1984 should have been Nigel's. Having qualified second behind Alain Prost, he went ahead after 11 laps when the Frenchman's McLaren was baulked by a spun car. But instead of adapting his pace to the conditions, Nigel seemed determined to extend his lead. After barely four more laps, he crashed into the guardrail going up the hill from Ste Devote. He has never denied making a mistake, although some of the blame was apportioned to the white line that he touched just before the car went out of control.

The Lotus 95T-Renault (above) was quick enough to win but let down too often by its fragile gearbox. The 'box broke again at Detroit (left), where the first start had to be abandoned after a multiple collision which was triggered when Nigel, starting third on the grid, attempted to squeeze his way past Piquet and Prost in front of him. He was subsequently fined and censured for rash driving, although he has always denied the charges.

F1 FOOTBALLERS The venue is a charity match held during the weekend of the 1984 San Marino GP. On the back row are Bellof, Patrese, Mansell, de Cesaris, Cecotto, Alboreto, Cheever (masked) and Winkelhock; in front are de Angelis, Alliot, Warwick and Senna.

It was at the Dutch GP of 1984 that Lotus boss Peter Warr informed the press that he had chosen Ayrton Senna to lead the Lotus team in 1985 and would therefore be letting Nigel go. The race would throw some temporary doubt on Warr's decision, for Nigel had perhaps his best race of the season, pushing through from a lowly 12th place at the start to pass his team-mate de Angelis and claim a storming third by the finish. But the season ended, as it had begun, with a string of retirements. Nigel was already looking to rejuvenating his career with Williams.

WILLIAMS

1985 – 1988

Frank Williams has admitted that when he invited Nigel to drive one of his Honda-powered cars in 1985, he expected the man from Birmingham to be a solid number two rather than a regular race winner. By the end of the year, as Keke Rosberg was to find out, Nigel had other ideas. Rosberg's replacement, Nelson Piquet, already had two titles to his name, yet he, too, discovered in 1986 that Mansell would move aside for nobody. Frank's injuries in a road car accident in March 1986 kept him away from racing for four months, allowing the feud between his drivers to fester. It even triggered Nigel's famously premature announcement of his retirement from F1. At the end of 1986, Williams' 'fair play' policy of not favouring either man arguably cost the team an almost certain drivers' title. Mansell would point out that his chances were wrecked by a famous blow-out at Adelaide. British race fans will remember that Piquet was beaten by Mansell to a couple of wins in 1987, but it was the Brazilian's consistency which carried him to title number three.

RIGHT The colour scheme was unmistakable, and the old-fashioned race number ("Red Five!" as Murray Walker labelled it) would become beloved of British race fans. Here at Spa-Francorchamps, in the Belgian GP of 1986, Nigel takes his Williams-Honda FW11 to the first of five victories in a season that would see him finish runner-up behind Alain Prost in the world championship.

Soon to be an object of public adulation, Nigel felt comfortable at Williams. At the first race of 1985, in Brazil, he chats (upper left) with long-time admirer and team manager Peter Collins, with Frank Williams listening in. But although he qualified fifth, he was forced to retire following a tangle (lower left) at the first corner with Michele Alboreto's Ferrari. Alboreto, who survived to finish the race second, bitterly insisted that he had been ahead when their wheels touched.

NEXT PAGE The breakthrough GP win, at his 72nd attempt, could hardly have come at a better place than Brands Hatch, in the European GP on 6 October 1985. Here, at the start, Senna's Lotus-Renault (12) leads into Paddock Bend from pole position. Several ferocious battles ensued, notably between Senna, Nelson Piquet and Keke Rosberg. It was when Rosberg baulked Senna after replacing a damaged tyre that Nigel was able to find a way past the Brazilian, who had been given his place at Lotus only 12 months earlier.

Nigel acknowledges the reception from the Brands Hatch faithful as he crosses the line (left) to take his first victory in a championship race. His winning margin over Ayrton Senna was a thoroughly satisfying 21 seconds. The Moët flows on the podium, with Senna almost hidden in the spray.

Kyalami made it two in a row for Nigel when he won the 1985 South African GP. Here he makes a great start from pole position, while team-mate Rosberg gets trapped in the pack. The Finn, well aware that Mansell had been under-rated until now, would make a storming come-back.

Pre-race briefing (above) as Nigel and Keke talk with Frank Williams at Kyalami. The Williams FW10 (below) had improved greatly, thanks to a more 'driveable' engine supplied by Honda. On the podium (right) Nigel bestows a greeting as Keke – who had finished second despite a big spin on dropped oil – awaits the presentation of the trophies.

At 0.014 second, the gap that separated race winner Ayrton Senna's Lotus-Renault from Nigel's charging Williams-Honda at Jérez in 1986 was officially the narrowest ever. Having made a late stop for tyres, Nigel's thoughts on the podium (left) were about how much better the race would have been if it had been one lap longer. No longer team-mates (right) but still friends: Nigel chats with Elio de Angelis, who would die only a few weeks later when his Brabham-BMW crashed during a test in France.

A sombre moment at Spa in May 1986 as Nigel bows his head in tribute to Elio de Angelis, who had lost his life only ten days earlier. Ayrton Senna is more than happy with his trophy for second place. Nigel relished the Belgian circuit and the dramatic swerve at Eau Rouge (right), and on this occasion benefited when the engine in team-mate Nelson Piquet's car expired while leading.

The Paul Ricard circuit, close to the holiday beaches of Provence, held some grim memories for Nigel in 1986. In March, Frank Williams had been gravely injured as he hurried away from a test here, and in May Elio de Angelis had been killed while testing. But Nigel stormed on, holding Prost's McLaren in second place.

NEXT PAGE The 1986 British GP gave Nigel his second consecutive Brands Hatch victory, albeit a lucky one. His car broke a drive shaft at the start, only for the race to be red-flagged after a serious first-lap crash involving Jacques Laffite. Driving the spare Williams at the re-start, Nigel duelled with team-mate Piquet and was able – just – to hold off the Brazilian by defending hard as he returned to the track after a pit stop. Here the two Williams drivers lead away at the first start, Piquet on pole.

NO FLASH PHOTOGRAPHY
PLEASE

E VIETATO IL FLASH
GRAZIE

PRIERE DE NE PAS
UTILISER DE FLASH
MERCI

KEINE BLITZ-FOTOS MACHEN
BITTE

With the 1986 drivers' world championship developing into a four-way fight, Bernie Ecclestone organised this photo call (above) for the four contenders at Brands Hatch. Nigel made himself less than popular with the photographers (left) when he and his doctor, Rafael Grajales (dark glasses), banned flash guns in the pits, owing to possible impairment of his vision. But 'Red Five' was urged on by the public as he battled in the race with Piquet.

Heading for victory at Brands Hatch in 1986 (above), with team-mate Nelson Piquet close behind. On the podium (right), the Brazilian does not look entirely happy about having to settle for the runner-up spot.

Hungary's first championship GP, in 1986, was to provide a Brazilian 1-2, with Nelson Piquet driving his Williams round the outside of Ayrton Senna's Lotus in a memorable move at the first corner. Nigel couldn't match Piquet and this moment (left) was about as close as he got to Senna. In fact, Piquet had found a transmission 'tweak' which he and his engineer kept secret from the other side of the garage. It was yet another incident in a team spat which would occupy team owner Frank Williams (above, with drivers) after his return to the team from injury.

The 1986 world championship was destined to slip from Nigel's grasp in the final round, in Australia, when, on lap 64 of the 82-lap race, a tyre failure on the main straight sidelined him dramatically and allowed Alain Prost to take the honours. The new street circuit in Adelaide was picturesque but unforgiving, and Nigel was lucky to escape unhurt. Throughout the year he had become close to James Hunt (right), the public school educated playboy who had won the 1976 world title at McLaren. Having retired in 1979, Hunt attended most GPs in his new role as a 'colour' commentator on F1 for BBC TV.

There was a turning point for the Piquet/Mansell relationship in 1987 at Imola, where the Brazilian crashed heavily at the Tamburello corner on Friday after another Goodyear tyre failure and was unable to take part in the race. There was much concern about the tyres and it was a relief when Sunday's race ended (top), without further incident, with Nigel victorious from Ayrton Senna and Ferrari driver Michele Alboreto (upper right). Piquet soon returned, wily as ever but perhaps less aggressive than before, and Nigel would dish out several defeats, including this one at the French GP (right), where he started from pole.

The British papers had a phrase for it: 'Mansell Mania'. It first gripped the country in 1986 and took off in 1987 as British fans took their new hero to heart, with the inevitable turn-out on the occasion of the British GP at Silverstone. Nigel responded by occasionally joining the public (as here), even though he was regularly mobbed.

Nigel drew inspiration from his adoring British fans, and in return he gave them some of the most memorable moments of his career. One of them occurred at Silverstone in 1987, where he came back from an unscheduled tyre stop to hunt down team-mate Nelson Piquet and pass him, for the win, at Stowe corner. Both men were watching their fuel very closely, and Nigel – who ran out half way round his victory lap – cut it particularly fine. Sparks fly (left) from the titanium skid plates as Nigel makes up ground after Piquet had taken an early lead (above). From an all-Williams front row on the grid to the one-two finish, the local team gave the home crowd everything they could have hoped for that day.

Nelson Piquet has admitted that he deliberately set out to divide loyalties within Williams, to compensate for being the foreigner in a British team. He also devoted himself to testing engineering innovations, one of which was the prototype 'active' suspension system which he (alone) was running when he won the Italian GP in September 1987 (above), beating Senna and a chastened Nigel.

The Spanish GP, late in the 1987 season, started with an all-Williams front row. Piquet led from the start (above) but ran into handling problems with his 'active' suspension, leaving the win for Nigel (right). Tired of always having cameras pointed in his direction, Nigel turned the tables (left). Fortunately, he chose a sponsor's product...

After winning in Spain, Nigel needed wins in both of the remaining races if he was to catch
Piquet's points total. He did it in Mexico (upper left), but then disaster struck at Suzuka in
Japan, where a minor driving mistake in practice developed into a heavy crash, the hard
landing inflicting back injuries which prevented Nigel from racing and left him on the sick list
for many weeks to come. In terms of victories in 1987, Nelson trailed Nigel by 3-6, but Piquet's
seven second places helped him garner 76 points and allowed him to clinch his third world
championship; Nigel took 61 points to Senna's 57. But Nigel was now a paddock celebrity (left):
here he chats with FISA President Jean-Marie Balestre and Bernie Ecclestone (back to camera).
In the centre of the picture is Ferrari sporting director Marco Piccinini, with whom Nigel had
already started negotiations.

At the end of 1987, alarmed by the effect of Frank Williams' injuries on his team's future, Honda parted company with Williams a year earlier than agreed. Although he had been courted by Ferrari for the 1988 season, Nigel remained faithful to the British team, now forced to use non-turbo Judd V8 engines. It was a serious error of judgement by the driver, whose best efforts could produce only two second places, including this one (left) at Silverstone. On the podium (upper left) with race winner Ayrton Senna and third man Alessandro Nannini, he looks understandably exhausted. As journalists found (above), Nigel had difficulty in explaining his decision.

In 14 starts with the ill-fated Williams-Judd of 1988, Nigel failed to finish on no fewer than 12 occasions. Nevertheless, there were occasional moments of glory, notably at the sinuous Hungaroring (above), where he qualified second and briefly held that position behind Ayrton Senna's McLaren, now equipped with Honda power. In the same race he was at least able to ferry Gerhard Berger back to the pits. But Nigel needed a new start, and shaving off the famous moustache (right) symbolised that need.

In the Spanish GP of 1988 (above), Nigel pulled off his second miracle of the season by finishing second to Alain Prost's McLaren-Honda. He bade farewell to Williams – at least for the time being – at Adelaide (left), where he briefly challenged the leaders with the fragile Judd-powered Williams FW12.

FERRARI

1989 – 1990

Arriving at Ferrari less than a year after the Old Man had died, Nigel understandably felt it was his duty to lift the team out of the doldrums. Although Ferrari was armed for 1989 with an exceptionally advanced car which had taken almost three years to develop, and while an extraordinary debut victory in Brazil showed the tifosi what 'Il Leone' could do, ultimately the team lacked the reliability and consistency to get the job done. The arrival of the politically astute Alain Prost as Nigel's team-mate in 1990 upset the equilibrium inside the Scuderia and unnerved Nigel so badly that he had difficulty concentrating on his racing. The parting, as was getting to be the habit with him and his teams, was not a happy one.

RIGHT Ferrari's needle-nosed type 640, designed by the meticulous John Barnard, was an irresistible lure to Nigel after his 1988 season in the doldrums at Williams. The car, seen here in Portugal late in the year, was fast but infuriatingly unreliable.

Nigel received a rapturous welcome at Ferrari, where his engineer was to be the American Steve Nichols (above), previously with Prost and Senna at McLaren. Their first race together, at the Jacarepagua circuit near Rio de Janeiro, ended with the most remarkable result of his career. After repeated hydraulic failures in practice and qualifying, Nigel confidently booked an early flight back to Europe. But despite electrical problems (cured by changing the steering wheel during a tyre-change stop) and after a battle with Alain Prost's McLaren (right), the car came home in first place (below). In testing it had never completed a race distance without breaking down, and it failed to finish the next four races.

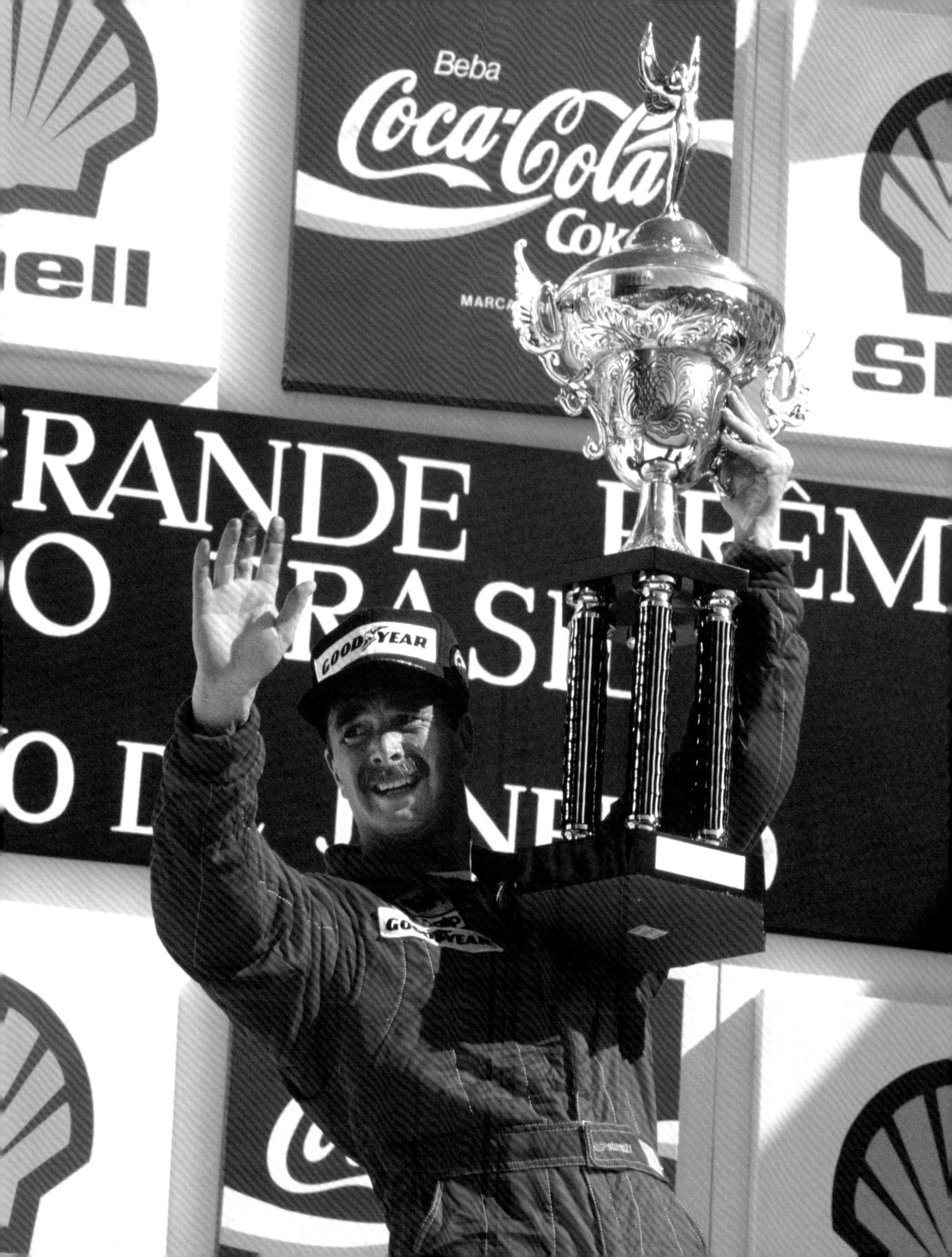
Beba
Coca-Cola
GOODYEAR

The glorious debut win with Ferrari had a painful conclusion on the podium (left), where Nigel cut his fingers as he grasped the sharp edges of the garish winner's trophy. Returning to Europe, the new Ferrari was continually dogged by failures in its innovative semi-automatic gearbox, which forced yet another retirement at Monaco (above) after Nigel had held third place.

NEXT PAGE This first-corner crash at the Paul Ricard circuit on the first lap of the French GP in 1989, caused by a late-braking Mauricio Gugelmin (upside down but unhurt), damaged the rear suspension of Nigel's race car. Although he took over Gerhard Berger's car, his mechanics lost time adjusting the car to fit him, and he had to take the re-start from pitlane. In a thrilling chase, and assisted by a few retirements, Nigel charged his way through the field and finally took second place – behind the McLaren-Honda of a distant Alain Prost – from Riccardo Patrese's Williams-Renault.

Nigel thoroughly enjoyed his first year at Ferrari, and his
fighting drive in France (upper left) added to his prestige
inside the team and reinforced his reputation with the
tifosi as 'Il Leone'. Although his attempts at learning their
language never really paid off, his Italian mechanics
loved and respected him. He remained close to Sheridan
Thynne (lower left), a long-time associate of Frank Williams
and someone who was always there with advice and
encouragement.

Nigel's second win for Ferrari did not come until August, at the Hungaroring (left), but it was well worth the wait. Tailing Senna's McLaren-Honda, he momentarily saw a chance to pass the Brazilian as they came up to lap the Onyx of Stefan Johansson. It was a breathtaking move, executed almost before he thought of it, but entirely legitimate, as Senna himself willingly agreed. And it was jubilantly celebrated by Nigel.

After Brazil and Hungary, Nigel was the toast of the Ferrari faithful. Some of them compared him with the much-missed Gilles Villeneuve, and a section of the grandstand at Monza (left) had no hesitation in declaring their affection. The architect of Ferrari's political strategy during Nigel's two years at Ferrari was the Scuderia's Direttore Sportive Cesare Fiorio (headphones, above), who – unknown to Nigel for several weeks – had been in negotiations with Alain Prost for the Frenchman to join the team in 1990.

The unreliability of the
Ferraris he had driven in 1989
had not been resolved in time
for the opening of the 1990
season, here in wet practice at
Phoenix, Arizona, USA. Once
again it was a transmission
problem which intervened,
causing Nigel to crash.

Nigel's successes with Ferrari in 1989 converted many thousands of British fans into banner-waving tifosi, and they flaunted their new loyalty at the British GP (above). By now he had set up his own Ferrari dealership, and he was allowed to show off the tyre-spinning potential of a road-going F40 at Silverstone. As a Special Constable on the Isle of Man, he would of course have frowned severely on such antics if they'd been performed on an open road.

The La Source hairpin at Spa, coming almost immediately after the start and requiring hard braking in the pack, has regularly been the scene of first-lap incidents. In 1990 Nigel was involved in this nose-crunching collision with the guardrail. With the car repaired, he took the re-start and finished third behind the McLarens of Senna and Prost.

The 1990 season at Ferrari, with Alain Prost as his team-mate, was to be a deeply unhappy one for Nigel. Not only did the revised type 641 continue to fail under him in more than half the races, but he became convinced that Prost was deliberately undermining his position inside the team. At Silverstone, where the type 641 retired yet again with transmission failure, he flabbergasted his fans by announcing that he would retire at the end of the year. Then, at the Portuguese GP (above), the car stayed healthy long enough for him to take an important victory which he celebrated (right) in the appropriate style.

The festering personal relationship between Nigel and Alain Prost, which at Silverstone had helped trigger the announcement of retirement at the end of 1990, was eventually resolved before the Spanish GP at Jérez. Nigel's confidence in his own bankability had been restored by Frank Williams, who even flew to the Isle of Man to persuade him to change his mind. With a new Williams contract on the table for 1991, Nigel decided to stay in F1. With his mind clear, he raced to second place in Spain, behind Prost, to whom he offered warm and seemingly genuine congratulations (above).

PREVIOUS PAGE Although the Ferrari type 641 was a development of the previous year's type 640, its designer, John Barnard, had quit Ferrari in the middle of the 1989 season. Both Barnard and Ferrari had become frustrated, for their own reasons, and the time was coming when Ferrari would have to accept that its traditional V12 engines were too big and thirsty as F1 cars shrank in size at the demands of influential aerodynamicists. Even so, the sight and sound of the 641 as it sparked its way round the world's race tracks (here, at Jérez in Spain) were enough to thrill anyone with a drop of petrol in his or her veins.

The last race of 1990, in Adelaide (above), found Nigel and the type 641 Ferrari in excellent form, and he finished second to Nelson Piquet's Benetton. It was a dignified and comfortable way for him to say goodbye to his short career as a Ferrari driver. He also made efforts, of a kind, to soothe his sometimes tortured relationship with the press. In an impromptu setting (left), he explains the reversal of his retirement plans to journalists – while wearing the headgear of his weekday job as a Special Constable.

WILLIAMS

1991 – 1992

Perhaps the greatest stroke of luck that Nigel enjoyed in the course of changing employers was that he found himself back at Williams in the two years when the British team was enjoying a golden period of technical superiority. Now with immaculately reliable and powerful engines from Renault, mounted in a chassis that bristled with technical innovations (including active suspension and an automatic gearbox), Williams was widely regarded by its rivals as unbeatable. Though the FW14 was seriously short of reliability in 1991, in FW14B form the car became untouchable in 1992, allowing Nigel to claim pole positions galore and to set records for unbroken runs of wins. He was unbeatable on points for the drivers' title with five races still to be contested, another record. But the dominance of the Williams/Renault combination attracted the interest of both Alain Prost and Ayrton Senna. Frank Williams' willingness to talk with the two champions unsettled Nigel, who once again concluded that he wasn't appreciated in F1 and headed off to race in America for 1993.

RIGHT Here on its way to victory at Silverstone, Nigel's Williams FW14-Renault thrills a capacity crowd with sparks from its titanium skid plates.

Although the Williams FW14 of 1991 was the fastest car of the season over a single lap, and its Renault V10 engine powerful and reliable, Nigel's hopes of becoming champion were destroyed by frailties of the chassis and a series of blunders during races, not all of them his responsibility. This was accepted by a harassed-looking technical boss Patrick Head (upper right), who had to wait until race 6, in Mexico (lower right), to celebrate a Williams 1-2, with an on-form Riccardo Patrese taking the win. Perhaps Nigel was still shattered by the after-effects of losing in Montreal (above), where he had dominated the Canadian GP until the engine died almost within sight of the flag. Williams insiders let it be known that he had been too busy waving to the crowd to downshift at the hairpin, which caused the French V10 to stall.

Chequered flag at last. The new home for the French GP in 1991 was Magny-Cours, a remote one-time club-racing circuit which had been expensively upgraded for F1. Nigel had a fight on his hands with Prost's Ferrari, but prevailed after passing the Frenchman twice. With nine races to go, his keenly anticipated duel with Senna and McLaren-Honda for the championship had started agonisingly late.

As always at home in England, Nigel drew extra strength from his fans, although his forays among them (left) now deteriorated into minor stampedes. On race day the crowd cheered their hero as he found a way past Senna and headed for what looked like an easy win, albeit worried in the closing laps by the return of some familiar gremlins. Senna's car ran out of fuel, though he was classified fourth after being ferried home by his old rival (above).

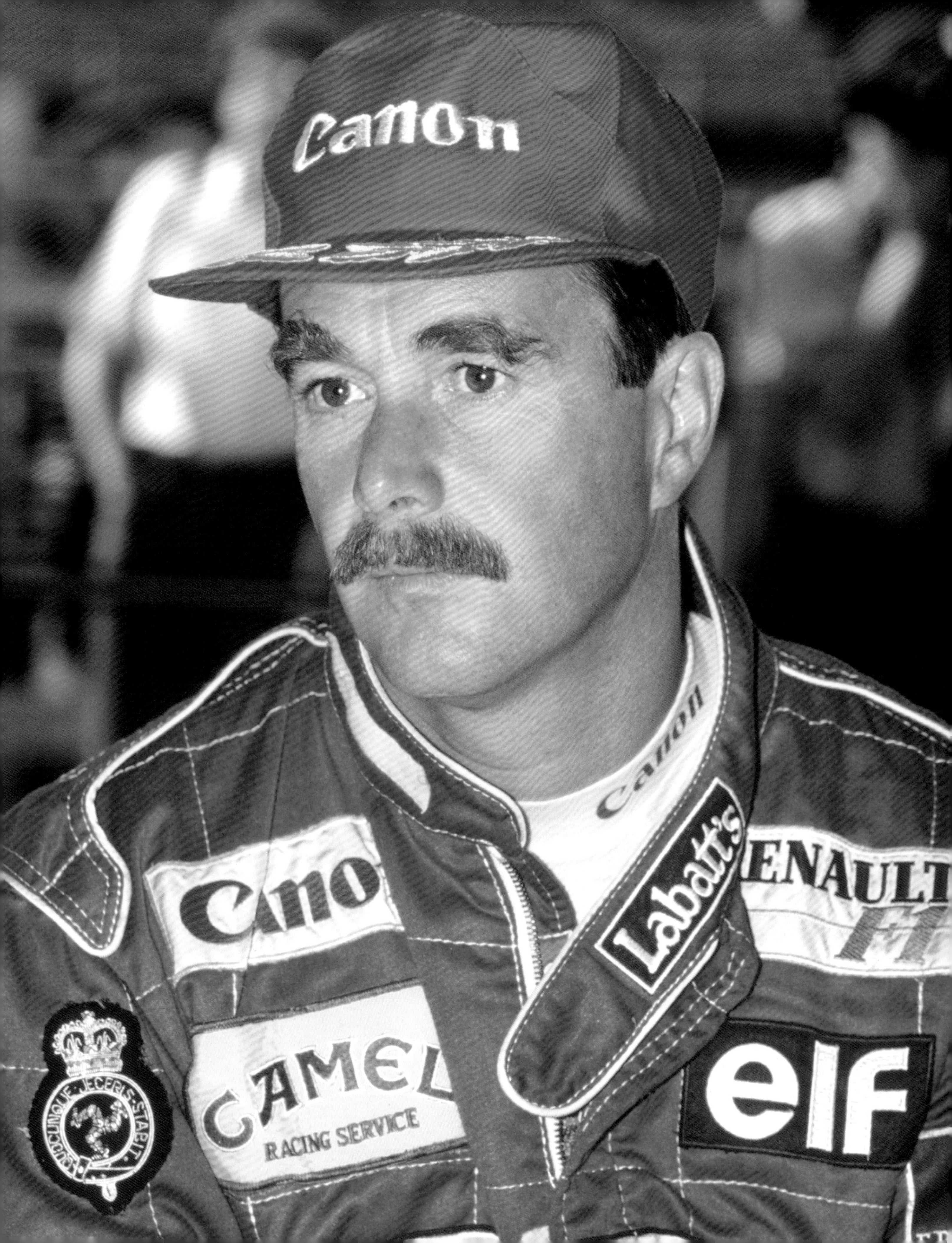
Canon
Canon
Canon
Labatt's
elf
RACING SERVICE

Combining the might of its 3.5-litre Renault V10 engine with active suspension and a semi-automatic gearbox, the Williams FW14 quickly proved to be the fastest combination of the 1991 season, if not always the most reliable. The brilliant engineer who headed the design department at the Williams HQ in Didcot was Adrian Newey, seen baffling Nigel with science.

The Italian GP in September found Nigel in majestic form, and after he had yet again disposed of Senna he took his fourth win of the season with a 16-second margin over the Brazilian. The unfortunate Patrese had led one lap until spinning out with more gearbox trouble. On the podium, Nigel is hailed by Senna and Prost – the three of them would take no fewer than eight world titles.

The Portuguese GP at Estoril produced a well-deserved
victory for a determined Riccardo Patrese, who started from
pole position and led Nigel from the start (above). But Nigel's
race was destined to end in ignominy when he was released
prematurely from a tyre-change pit stop and lost a wheel a
few metres down pitlane. Instead of pulling their car back into
the box, his crew refitted the wheel in pitlane, a clear breach
of the rules which earned Nigel a disqualification.

The Spanish GP of 1991 was contested on the splendid new Circuit de Catalunya at Montmeló, north of Barcelona. The long straight produced an iconic moment as Mansell and Senna, who had argued in the pre-race drivers' briefing, duelled for the lead. At close to 200mph both men kept their cool, and Nigel was able to power through. Senna spun off in the closing stages, almost taking Nigel with him, but the Englishman survived that scare and was cheered home by his crew (above).

Arriving in Japan, with just two races to go, Nigel had no more than an outside chance of taking the title from Senna. He challenged the Brazilian's McLaren for the first nine laps before running wide at the first corner (left), spinning off into the gravel and handing the title to his rival. Nigel explained that his brake pedal had gone soft.

NEXT PAGE Most Mansell fans will surely agree that he always looked most at home in a Williams. The FW14 of 1991 (seen here at Kyalami) was fast but not always reliable; its technical superiority attracted envious glances from every driver in the paddock. Both Ayrton Senna and Alain Prost knew that it promised them the best chance of winning in future, and eventually both would become Williams drivers. For the 1992 season, though, Frank Williams had already put his trust in true-Brit Nigel Mansell.

By the start of the 1992 season the engineers at Williams had found the cure for the technical shortcomings of 1991, presenting the new car as the 'B' version of the FW14. It was quick off the mark, allowing Nigel to win all of the first five races. In Mexico, the second round of the championship, he and Riccardo Patrese were followed home by the Benetton-Ford of Michael Schumacher. It was the first-ever podium appearance by the 23-year-old German newcomer.

Turn 1 at Interlagos in the Brazilian GP of 1992. Riccardo Patrese, from second place on the grid, has momentarily slipped ahead of Nigel, but he wouldn't stay there for long.

After the first race at Barcelona's new circuit in 1991, for 1992 the Spanish GP was moved to the beginning of the season. The weather was far from Mediterranean, although that made no difference to Nigel, who scored his fourth win from four starts. Even in the worst of the downpour (above), the FW14B's active suspension worked perfectly.

At Imola in 1992 (above), Nigel was already well on his way to the title. He took his fifth consecutive win of the season, beating Senna's 1991 record of four wins, and he was dutifully followed home by team-mate Riccardo Patrese. Only two other drivers were still on the same lap. On an unusually hot afternoon, Nigel was just one of several drivers who suffered on the hard-braking circuit. "The only thing that didn't work very good today was my body," he said. "I had cramp and muscle spasm down my right side and in my leg. That is because my brake pedal went hard, and maybe we had too much cooling on the discs." The successes of 1992 brought personal sponsorships flooding in, but Special Constable Nigel Mansell still found space on his overalls for an Isle of Man Police badge (right).

Everything looked good in May 1992 for Nigel to claim a much-coveted win at Monaco, and the family (wife Rosanne, daughter Chloe and sons Leo and Greg) were there to support him (above). He led away from pole position and was still in front with seven laps to go when a rear wheel nut came loose, forcing him to stop for a replacement rear wheel. Senna slipped his McLaren in front (right) and was not to be dislodged, despite Nigel's best efforts in his clearly faster Williams. He never returned to race in the Principality.

After an unscheduled stop to replace a rear wheel, Nigel sets off up the hill from Ste Devote in pursuit of Senna. Although the Englishman closed a 5sec gap in barely four laps, Senna used all his cunning to make passing impossible and to grab his fifth Monaco victory. On the podium (above), an exhausted Nigel wipes away the sweat. Despite his disappointment, he emphasised that Senna's driving had been tough but correct. Senna, though, was gloomy about his championship prospects with the V12-engined McLaren-Honda. "The Williams-Renault cars are much quicker than anybody, not only us," he said. "In the near future, I don't see the possibility of anyone matching their performance."

Qualifying for the French GP (above), Nigel took his seventh pole position in eight races. Approaching the start after the formation lap (right), he sees strong winds fluttering the flags and is confronted with a sky full of menace. The race started normally but was then red-flagged when a torrential rain storm flooded the track: after the re-start, on wet tyrres, Patrese waved Nigel through to let him take his sixth victory of the 1992 season. At home on the Isle of Man was a message of congratulations from three-times champion Jackie Stewart, whose record total of 27 GP victories had now been equalled by Nigel.

Togged up in period clothes for a Renault promotion with a vintage car, Nigel and Rosanne force a smile for the cameras. He looks a lot more at home in the company car (right), which was a winner regardless of weather conditions.

Pole man meets royalty: just before the start of the British GP, Nigel is introduced to the Duke of Kent and his extravagant beard. The race was a sell-out, with an estimated 120,000 spectators packing out Silverstone to share in yet another joyful Williams parade. At the start (right) the two Williams drivers were level, but an inspired Nigel was on the way to beating his team-mate by almost 40 seconds at the finish.

Heading down to Stowe corner on the first lap, Nigel has Patrese in his sights; within two corners he was in the lead. On the slowing-down lap (right), Nigel passes Ayrton Senna and his stationary McLaren-Honda, which had broken down with gearbox trouble. It was the end of any hopes that Senna had of challenging for the 1992 title.

As Nigel crossed the line (upper left) to win the British GP by almost 40 seconds from Patrese, hundreds of frenzied fans were already breaking down the barriers and pouring on to the track (lower left). On the slowing-down lap, when other drivers were still racing to the finish, Nigel's car was mobbed (above). As the crowds celebrated, though, Silverstone officials breathed a sigh of relief that the only casualty was one man whose foot had been run over. In future years the circuit was to impose a 90,000 limit on the number of race tickets sold.

Nigel shares the happiness of his Silverstone win with Rosanne (above), who had seen her husband announce his retirement at Silverstone two years earlier, only to change his mind. Now she knew it had been worth it. After showering his delirious supporters with champagne on the podium (right), Nigel thanked them for their help: "Every time I got on to the straight, all the fans blew – and my engine picked up about 300 revs! When the opposition came, they blew in the opposite direction – and slowed them down!"

The German GP at Hockenheim produced Nigel's eighth win of the 1992 season, but it was not without incident. The car jumped a gear at the start, which allowed Patrese into a brief lead; he felt the car sliding in the early laps and made a cautionary early stop for tyres; then he briefly spun down an escape road while trying to re-pass Senna's McLaren-Honda. Even so, Nigel was able to beat the Brazilian by four seconds, increasing his lead over Patrese in the drivers' championship to 46 points, with six races still to go.

NEXT PAGE Trying to concentrate before the start in Hungary, Nigel is surrounded by photographers and pressmen curious about his future. Frank Williams, knowing that Nigel had promised to retire if he won the title, was already negotiating with both Ayrton Senna and Alain Prost. Nigel, who may have forgotten that promise, felt betrayed and let it be known that he would only stay with Williams in 1993 if he was guaranteed number one status. "Frank Williams must offer me the [same] opportunity that I have had for the last two years," he said. "I don't want anything more than I have had before." He later accused Williams of making an offer which was then withdrawn. Meanwhile, he himself had started talking to Indycar team owner Carl Haas...

It took a second place for Nigel to do it, but the Hungarian GP was the race which put his points total in the 1992 championship out of reach of anybody else. Having qualified second behind Patrese, he lost two places to the McLaren drivers at the start. When Patrese lost time with a spin, Nigel was lining up Senna for the lead but was called in to replace a deflating Goodyear, dropping him to sixth place. In a typically aggressive come-back drive, he was able to pick off everyone in front of him except Senna (upper left). Yet again there were errant fans on the track on the slow-down lap (above).

The 1992 world champion's celebrations begin (left). At the time, Nigel was unaware that Senna, with him on the podium in Hungary, had made it known that he would be prepared to drive for Williams in 1993 for no fee. On this special day, Rosanne was invited by the FIA to sit in on the post-race press conference (above).

The end of Nigel's championship year was marked by three retirements in four races. The exception was at the Estoril circuit in Portugal, where he scored a crushing 37-second victory over Gerhard Berger's McLaren-Honda. At the start the two Williams drivers are level, but Riccardo Patrese's race ended in a big crash.

On the way to his final victory of the 1992 season with
Williams-Renault, in Portugal (above), Nigel passes the
wrecked FW14B of team-mate Patrese, who had crashed
heavily after a misunderstanding with McLaren driver Gerhard
Berger. In Japan (upper right), Nigel rather grudgingly agreed
to help Patrese by waving him through, only for his engine to
blow up. Nigel's Australian GP (lower right) ended after he and
Senna tangled on lap 19 and retired.

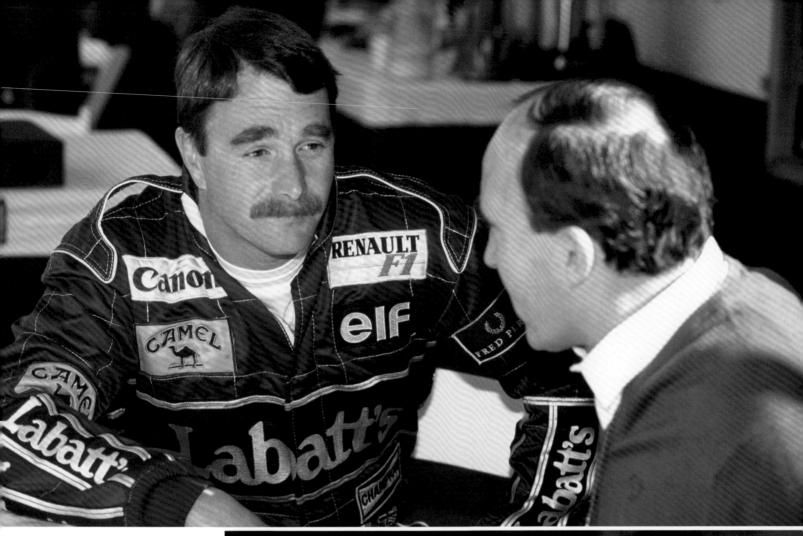

As soon as it became clear that Nigel's threats about going to race in America were serious, a tabloid newspaper rustled up some banners and a couple of models to make a rather muddled protest outside the Williams factory at Didcot (upper left). Their antics cut no ice with Frank Williams himself (above), who had made up his mind to end the partnership. But the two men buried their differences when they went to Paris to pick up their trophies at the FIA prize-giving in December (left). There was also the inevitable appearance at Madame Tussaud's wax museum in London (right).

TO THE USA

1993 – 1994

The Mansell family had already decided to make Florida home when Nigel started talking to the Indycar team co-owned by Chicago businessman Carl Haas and actor Paul Newman. The transition to the heavier cars presented no difficulties, but what was really surprising was Nigel's ability to make himself at home on the terrifyingly fast ovals, albeit after he'd hurt his back while qualifying for his first race on the 'banks'. At first the relationship with long-standing Newman-Haas driver Mario Andretti seemed cordial enough, and the American felt no rancour when Nigel started to build a championship-winning points tally. But in 1994, with a car that was outclassed almost everywhere, the two men started to fall out as a result of clashes both on the track and off it. Feeling unloved again, Nigel was greatly reassured when he got a call asking him to consider rejoining Williams.

RIGHT Having won the Indycar title in 1993 with the Lola entered by Carl Haas and Paul Newman, Nigel was entitled to carry number 1 on his car in 1994. But the new Lola was no match for the resurgent Penskes and the team didn't have a single victory to celebrate.

Right from the start, Nigel felt comfortable in an Indycar, despite its turbo engine and much greater weight than an F1 car. Testing the Newman-Haas Lola at Sebring (above) and at the short Phoenix oval early in 1993, he set record-breaking times. He went on to win the first Indycar round, at the Surfers Paradise street circuit in Australia, on his début outing. But on his return to Phoenix in April (right) he crashed heavily and was too badly knocked about to race; victory went to his team-mate Mario Andretti. Nigel had learned the hard way how dangerous the ovals can be.

Still in pain from the back injury suffered in his Phoenix shunt, Nigel found that Long Beach (above and left) had changed considerably since he last raced an F1 car there in 1983. He finished third behind Canadian Paul Tracy (Penske, 12) and American Bobby Rahal. Before the next race, the Indianapolis 500 (right), he underwent surgery to repair the damage to his back.

Despite being unfamiliar with the ritual and pomp (left) of the Indy '500', Nigel had no difficulty with his Rookie test and found that his Newman-Haas Lola was competitive with the top qualifiers. He led the race at three different stages and came back strongly after losing time when he overshot his pit while refuelling. He was lying third (right) with seven laps to go when he smacked the wall, which brought out the yellow flags. Although his car was still strong, he fumbled the re-start when race leader Emerson Fittipaldi cannily slowed the field behind him as the race went green again. Nigel was caught napping with his turbo on low boost and had to be content with third place behind Fittipaldi and Arie Luyendijk.

With a large house in sunny Clearwater, Florida, and with few
of the media pressures which had been forced on Nigel as an
F1 driver, life for the Mansell family in America was more than
comfortable. Chloe, Greg and Leo (right) were often there to
support their father at the races as he stormed his way to five
victories and the overall crown in the grandly named PPG Indycar
World Series. One of the few races in which his car failed to
complete the distance in 1993 was in Toronto (above).

Victory in the penultimate race of the season, on the short oval at Nazareth (above), gave Nigel an unassailable points lead in the PPG championship. He hoists the trophy (left) at the Pennsylvania track, local stamping ground for his team-mate Mario Andretti. He was destined not to finish the final round, at the Laguna Seca road circuit in northern California (right), after a collision with a backmarker's car.

NEXT PAGE Refuelling has been a feature of American racing from the very earliest days. Here at Laguna Seca the Newman-Haas crew get down to work before Nigel retired. Note the Mansell helmets.

Back in England in October 1993, fulfilling a
Ford promotion during the weekend of the
British Touring Car shoot-out at Donington Park,
Nigel made time (left) for a US-style autograph
signing session with his British fans. Well over
60,000 of them turned out to meet him.

The TOCA shoot-out at Donington Park was a special televised touring car event, with Nigel having to adapt himself to the intricacies of a front-wheel-drive Ford Mondeo (above). The car's engine developed a misfire during the race, and it was while he was defending himself against Tiff Needell's Vauxhall Cavalier that Nigel crashed heavily, sustaining some bruising.

Back with the Newman-Haas team in America for 1994,
carrying the champion's number 1, a pensive Nigel found that
his Lola T94/00 was no match for the latest Penske in the hands
of Tracy, Fittipaldi and Unser Jr. To make things worse, relations
with team-mate Mario Andretti (above) became strained.

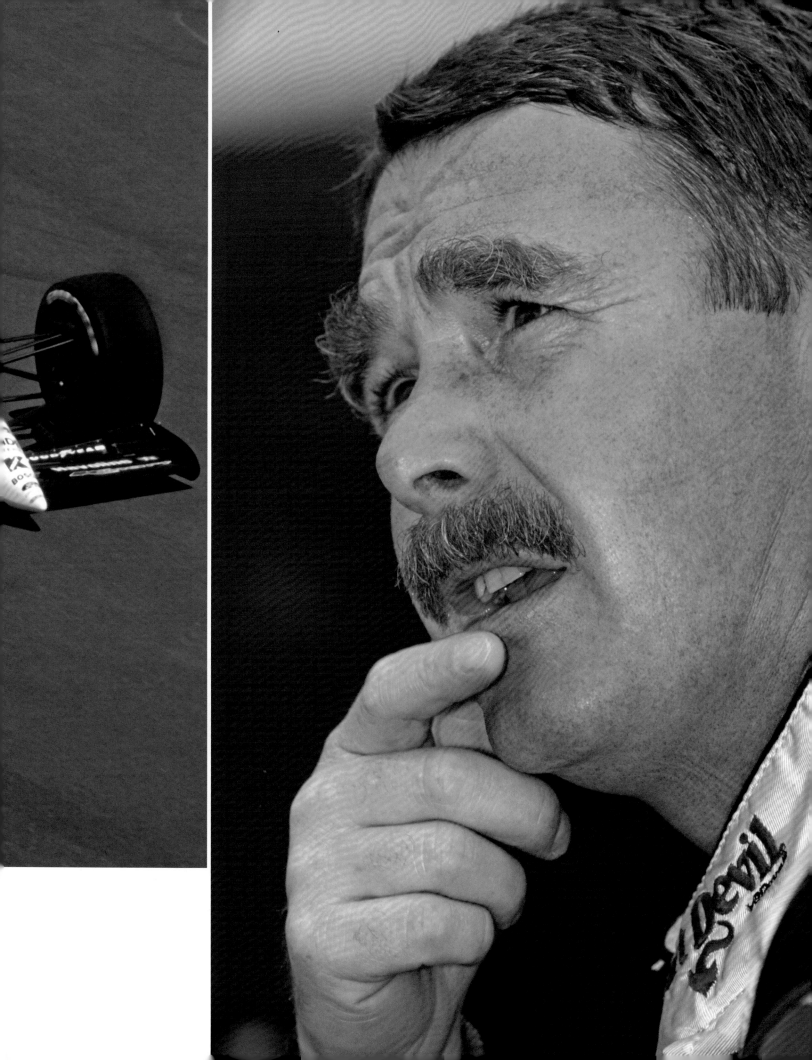

At Indianapolis in 1994, Nigel poses on the start line (upper left) and gets a hug from co-owner Paul Newman (lower left). In the race (above) he was running as high as third place, only to be eliminated during a yellow-flag period when a semi-professional driver misjudged his speed and ran over the top of the Lola. The incident brought home to Nigel the dangers presented by high-speed oval racing.

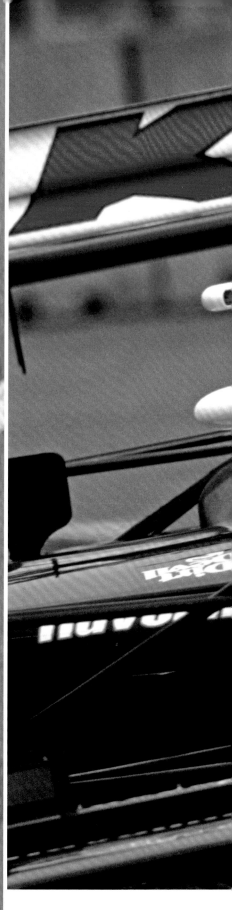

The 1994 season of Indycar racing yielded no wins and only three podium finishes for Nigel. The love affair with American racing had faded. With F1 opportunities opening up for him again, he decided on a return to Europe.

SWANSONG

It was not the happiest of circumstances in which to return to F1, but a man as sensitive as Nigel could surely only feel vindicated in knowing that it was his number that Bernie Ecclestone called when Williams needed to fill the place of Ayrton Senna after that horrible weekend at Imola in May 1994. At 41, and with two years of good living in Florida behind him, Nigel wasn't in such good physical condition as two and a half years before. He was also not race 'sharp', and he was prone to making quite serious mistakes in his driving. The Williams management hadn't been convinced it was the right move to take Nigel back, but Damon Hill was delighted to have someone of his countryman's class to help him in his bid for the drivers' title. Williams decided against making Nigel an offer for 1995. And the less said about his two races with McLaren-Mercedes that year, the better...

RIGHT From the start of the 1994 season, the Williams FW16-Renault had been a difficult car to drive. Some major changes were being made around the time that Nigel joined the team for the French GP in June, and he confirmed Damon Hill's verdict that they made a significant improvement.

Nigel would not have returned to F1 with Williams-Renault at the French GP in July 1994 without the personal intervention of Bernie Ecclestone, who discreetly negotiated a four-race contract and even helped to fund the deal. With minimum pre-race running, Nigel was understandably outperformed at Magny-Cours by his team-mate Damon Hill (above), who took pole position and finished the race in second place behind the Benetton-Ford of Michael Schumacher (left). Nigel got up to third place before his transmission failed.

Relieved to have put a sometimes acrimonious Indycar season behind him, Nigel returned to Williams-Renault for the last three races of the 1994 season. He crashed out in Portugal and took a gritty fourth place in Japan before triumphing in the final race of the season at Adelaide in Australia (left and above). Starting from pole position, he tapped a wall on the first lap and saw Damon Hill and Michael Schumacher go past in their battle for the drivers' championship. After both had been eliminated in Schumacher's controversial collision with his English rival, Nigel battled his way past Gerhard Berger's Ferrari to win.

Celebrating on the Adelaide podium with his friend Gerhard Berger, Nigel could reflect on having capped his GP comeback with a victory, 15 seasons on from his F1 début. At 41, he could start thinking – again – about retiring, but he was already giving serious thought to pushing on for one more year. When pressed (right) by journalists in Australia, though, he was not prepared to comment.

In a move which most pundits regarded as a gamble on both sides, Nigel had to endure some good-natured taunts about his age and weight. Nevertheless, he had already decided to sign up for 1995 with McLaren-Mercedes boss Ron Dennis. One of the driver's quips at the launch of the new McLaren (above) in London was that "if it goes as well as it looks, it will be a winner". The MP4/10B was one of the ugliest McLarens ever, and its performance on the track also fell short.

In his second race in the McLaren MP4/10B, at Barcelona (above), Nigel found the handling impossible and parked it. After 187 GPs and 31 victories, this atypical gesture marked the end of his career in top-line motor racing. In discussions with senior Williams engineer Adrian Newey (right), they were probably not making jokes about the McLaren's cramped cockpit, which forced Nigel to miss two GPs while a more capacious chassis was made for him.

NEXT PAGE Doing his best with the much-maligned McLaren MP4/10B at Barcelona in what was to be his final F1 appearance, Nigel had to concede defeat. The Anglo-German team persevered with the car, allowing Mika Häkkinen to salvage two second places with it later in the season.

The appeal of the Grand Prix Masters series proved irresistible to Nigel, who came out of retirement to join a group of other GP veterans in the 650hp single-seater cars and stylishly won the first of them, at Kyalami in South Africa, in November 2005. Throughout the race the 51-year-old Englishman battled with two times world champion Emerson Fittipaldi, then aged 58. On the podium (right) they were joined by Nigel's one-time Williams partner Riccardo Patrese.

On a warm summer's evening in 2005, the streets of London's West End were closed so that a handful of current F1 cars could be 'demonstrated' ahead of a possible world championship Grand Prix in the city. Nigel agreed to drive a current-model Jordan (left), making friends with a handful of policemen (above). London Mayor Ken Livingstone decided that F1 would be too expensive for London, so he threw his support instead behind a bid for the 2012 Olympic Games...

As a passionate golfer, Nigel tried to persuade sons Leo and Greg (above) to take up the game professionally – but in 2006 they decided they preferred to race cars. Nigel managed their efforts in that year's Formula BMW Championship, then returned to racing himself in 2007 in the Tourist Trophy race at Silverstone. He enjoyed co-driving this privately entered Ferrari 430 (left) to seventh in class and told the press (right) that he was considering some more outings in the GT category.

RACE RESULTS

Compiled by David Hayhoe

1976

Date	Country/event	Circuit	Race no.	Car	Model	Engine	Configuration	Notes	Grid position	Result
29/05	UK	Mallory Park	-	Hawke	DL11	Ford	4	fastest lap	-	1
10/07	UK	Castle Combe	-	Hawke	DL11	Ford	4	fastest lap	-	1
10/07	UK	Castle Combe	-	Hawke	DL11	Ford	4		-	6
12/08	UK	Castle Combe	-	Hawke	DL11	Ford	4		-	1
17/08	UK	Oulton Park	-	Hawke	DL11	Ford	4	fastest lap	-	1
17/08	UK	Oulton Park	-	Hawke	DL11	Ford	4	fastest lap	-	1
19/08	UK	Mallory Park	-	Hawke	DL11	Ford	4	fastest lap	-	2

1977

Date	Country/event	Circuit	Race no.	Car	Model	Engine	Configuration	Notes	Grid position	Result
06/03	UK	Silverstone	-	Javelin	JL5	Ford	4	transmission/pole	-	dns
13/03	UK	Oulton Park	-	Javelin	JL5	Ford	4		-	3
13/03	UK	Oulton Park	-	Javelin	JL5	Ford	4		-	3
20/03	UK	Silverstone	-	Javelin	JL5	Ford	4	fastest lap	-	2
20/03	UK	Silverstone	-	Javelin	JL5	Ford	4	fastest lap	-	2
27/03	UK	Snetterton	-	Javelin	JL5	Ford	4		-	3
27/03	UK	Snetterton	-	Javelin	JL5	Ford	4	reason unknown	-	ret
03/04	UK	Silverstone	-	Javelin	JL5	Ford	4		-	5
10/04	UK	Snetterton	-	Javelin	JL5	Ford	4		-	4
11/04	UK	Thruxton	-	Javelin	JL5	Ford	4		-	2
01/05	UK	Brands Hatch	-	Javelin	JL5	Ford	4	fastest lap	-	1
01/05	UK	Brands Hatch	-	Javelin	JL5	Ford	4		-	3
07/05	UK	Oulton Park	-	Javelin	JL5	Ford	4	rear suspension	-	ret
08/05	UK	Thruxton	-	Crosslé	25F	Ford	4	fastest lap	-	1
15/05	UK	Silverstone	-	Crosslé	25F	Ford	4	1 minute penalty	-	nc
22/05	UK	Oulton Park	-	Crosslé	25F	Ford	4	fastest lap	-	1
22/05	UK	Oulton Park	-	Crosslé	25F	Ford	4	engine	-	ret
23/05	UK	Brands Hatch	-	Crosslé	25F	Ford	4	fastest lap	-	1
23/05	UK	Brands Hatch	-	Crosslé	25F	Ford	4	accident	-	ret
24/07	UK	Brands Hatch	-	Crosslé	32F	Ford	4	fastest lap	-	2
24/07	UK	Brands Hatch	-	Crosslé	32F	Ford	4		-	4
31/07	UK	Donington Park	-	Crosslé	32F	Ford	4	fastest lap	-	1
31/07	UK	Donington Park	-	Crosslé	32F	Ford	4	fastest lap	-	1
07/08	UK	Donington Park	-	Crosslé	32F	Ford	4		-	2
07/08	UK	Donington Park	-	Crosslé	32F	Ford	4		-	1
20/08	UK	Oulton Park	-	Crosslé	32F	Ford	4		-	3
20/08	UK	Oulton Park	-	Crosslé	32F	Ford	4		-	3
21/08	UK	Mallory Park	-	Crosslé	32F	Ford	4	fastest lap	-	1
21/08	UK	Mallory Park	-	Crosslé	32F	Ford	4	fastest lap	-	1
27/08	UK	Donington Park	-	Puma	377	Toyota	4	reason unknown	-	ret
27/08	UK	Donington Park	-	Crosslé	32F	Ford	4	fastest lap	-	1
27/08	UK	Donington Park	-	Crosslé	32F	Ford	4	fastest lap	-	2
29/08	UK	Silverstone	-	Puma	377	Toyota	4	reason unknown	-	ret
29/08	UK	Silverstone	-	Crosslé	32F	Ford	4	fastest lap	-	1
29/08	UK	Silverstone	-	Crosslé	32F	Ford	4		-	2
04/09	UK	Mallory Park	-	Crosslé	32F	Ford	4	fastest lap	-	1
04/09	UK	Mallory Park	-	Crosslé	32F	Ford	4		-	1
11/09	UK	Donington Park	-	Crosslé	32F	Ford	4	fastest lap	-	2
11/09	UK	Donington Park	-	Crosslé	32F	Ford	4		-	1
18/09	UK	Silverstone	-	Crosslé	32F	Ford	4		-	2
24/09	UK	Oulton Park	-	Crosslé	32F	Ford	4	fastest lap	-	1
24/09	UK	Oulton Park	-	Crosslé	32F	Ford	4	fastest lap	-	1
01/10	UK	Silverstone	-	Lola	T570	Toyota	4		-	4
01/10	UK	Silverstone	-	Crosslé	32F	Ford	4	fastest lap	-	1
02/10	UK	Donington Park	-	Crosslé	32F	Ford	4	fastest lap	-	1
30/10	UK	Thruxton	-	Lola	T570	Toyota	4		-	10
30/10	UK	Thruxton	-	Crosslé	32F	Ford	4	fastest lap	-	1
06/11	UK	Brands Hatch	-	Crosslé	32F	Ford	4	accident	-	ret
13/11	UK	Thruxton	-	Lola	T570	Toyota	4		-	5
13/11	UK	Thruxton	-	Crosslé	32F	Ford	4		-	1

1978

Date	Country/event	Circuit	Race no.	Car	Model	Engine	Configuration	Notes	Grid position	Result
19/03	UK	Silverstone	-	March	783	Toyota	4		-	2
27/03	UK	Thruxton	-	March	783	Toyota	4		-	7
16/04	UK	Brands Hatch	-	March	783	Toyota	4		-	7
22/04	UK	Oulton Park	-	March	783	Toyota	4		-	7
30/04	UK	Donington Park	-	March	783	Toyota	4		-	4
25/06	UK	Donington Park	-	Chevron	B42	Hart	4		-	dnq

1979

Date	Country/event	Circuit	Race no.	Car	Model	Engine	Configuration	Notes	Grid position	Result
04/03	UK	Silverstone	-	March	783/793	Triumph	4		-	11
11/03	UK	Thruxton	-	March	783/793	Triumph	4		-	2
25/03	UK	Silverstone	-	March	783/793	Triumph	4	1st place car disqualified	-	1
01/04	UK	Snetterton	-	March	783/793	Triumph	4		-	8
08/04	UK	Donington Park	-	March	783/793	Triumph	4		-	7
16/04	UK	Thruxton	-	March	783/793	Triumph	4		-	4
07/05	UK	Brands Hatch	-	March	783/793	Triumph	4		-	6
20/05	UK	Donington Park	-	March	783/793	Triumph	4		-	6
20/05	UK	Donington Park	-	March	783/793	Triumph	4	accident	-	ret
26/05	Monaco	Monte Carlo	-	March	783/793	Triumph	4		-	11
10/06	UK	Brands Hatch	-	March	783/793	Triumph	4		-	4
17/06	UK	Cadwell Park	-	March	783/793	Triumph	4	shock absorber/tyres	-	ret
01/07	UK	Silverstone	-	March	783/793	Triumph	4		-	8
14/07	UK	Silverstone	-	March	783/793	Triumph	4		-	6
27/08	UK	Silverstone	-	March	783/793	Triumph	4		-	6
09/09	UK	Donington Park	-	March	783/793	Triumph	4		-	2
15/09	UK	Oulton Park	-	March	783/793	Triumph	4	accident/broken vertebrae	-	ret
28/10	UK	Thruxton	-	March	783/793	Triumph	4		-	8
03/11	UK	Thruxton	-	March	783/793	Triumph	4	engine	-	ret

1980

Date	Country/event	Circuit	Race no.	Car	Model	Engine	Configuration	Notes	Grid position	Result
02/03	UK	Silverstone	-	March	803	Toyota	4		5	4
09/03	UK	Thruxton	-	March	803	Toyota	4		5	4
30/03	UK	Brands Hatch	12	March	803	Toyota	4	fastest lap	6	4
07/04	UK	Thruxton	-	March	803	Toyota	4		7	5
20/04	UK	Silverstone	-	March	803	Toyota	4		9	6
05/05	UK	Thruxton	-	March	803	Toyota	4	engine	7	r
11/05	UK	Snetterton	-	March	803	Toyota	4		5	6
17/05	Monaco	Monte Carlo	33	March	803	Toyota	4		7	8
26/05	UK	Silverstone	-	March	803	Toyota	4		6	6
08/06	UK	Silverstone	34	Ralt	RH6	Honda	V6		14	11
22/06	Belgium	Zolder	34	Ralt	RH6	Honda	V6	accident	9	r
20/07	Netherlands	Zandvoort	34	Ralt	RH6	Honda	V6		6	5
17/08	AUSTRIA	Österreichring	43	Lotus	81B	Ford Cosworth	V8	engine	24	r
31/08	NETHERLANDS	Zandvoort	43	Lotus	81B	Ford Cosworth	V8	brakes/accident	16	r
14/09	ITALY	Imola	43	Lotus	81B	Ford Cosworth	V8			nq
28/09	Germany	Hockenheim	26	Ralt	RH6	Honda	V6		2	2

1981

Date	Country/event	Circuit	Race no.	Car	Model	Engine	Configuration	Notes	Grid position	Result
07/02	South Africa	Kyalami	12	Lotus	81	Ford Cosworth	V8	non-championship	8	10
15/03	USA West	Long Beach	12	Lotus	81	Ford Cosworth	V8	accident	7	r
29/03	BRAZIL	Rio de Janeiro	12	Lotus	81	Ford Cosworth	V8		13	11
12/04	ARGENTINA	Buenos Aires No.15	12	Lotus	81	Ford Cosworth	V8	engine	15	r
17/05	BELGIUM	Zolder	12	Lotus	81	Ford Cosworth	V8		10	3
31/05	MONACO	Monte Carlo	12	Lotus	87	Ford Cosworth	V8	rear suspension	3	r
21/06	SPAIN	Jarama	12	Lotus	87	Ford Cosworth	V8		11	6
05/07	FRANCE	Dijon Prenois	12	Lotus	87	Ford Cosworth	V8		13	7
18/07	BRITAIN	Silverstone	12	Lotus	87	Ford Cosworth	V8			nq
02/08	GERMANY	Hockenheim	12	Lotus	87	Ford Cosworth	V8	fuel leak	15	r
16/08	AUSTRIA	Österreichring	12	Lotus	87	Ford Cosworth	V8	engine	11	r
30/08	NETHERLANDS	Zandvoort	12	Lotus	87	Ford Cosworth	V8	electrics	17	r
13/09	ITALY	Monza	12	Lotus	87	Ford Cosworth	V8	handling	12	r
27/09	CANADA	Montréal	12	Lotus	87	Ford Cosworth	V8	accident	5	r
17/10	USA CAESARS PALACE	Las Vegas	12	Lotus	87	Ford Cosworth	V8		9	4

1982

Date	Country/event	Circuit	Race no.	Car	Model	Engine	Configuration	Notes	Grid position	Result
23/01	SOUTH AFRICA	Kyalami	12	Lotus	87B	Ford Cosworth	V8	electrics	18	r
21/03	BRAZIL	Rio de Janeiro	12	Lotus	91	Ford Cosworth	V8		14	3
04/04	USA West	Long Beach	12	Lotus	91	Ford Cosworth	V8		17	7
09/05	BELGIUM	Zolder	12	Lotus	91	Ford Cosworth	V8	clutch	7	r
23/05	MONACO	Monte Carlo	12	Lotus	91	Ford Cosworth	V8		11	4
06/06	USA	Detroit	12	Lotus	91	Ford Cosworth	V8	engine	7	r
13/06	CANADA	Montréal	12	Lotus	91	Ford Cosworth	V8	accident/injury	14	r
18/07	BRITAIN	Brands Hatch	12	Lotus	91	Ford Cosworth	V8	driver discomfort	23	r
08/08	GERMANY	Hockenheim	12	Lotus	91	Ford Cosworth	V8		18	9
15/08	AUSTRIA	Österreichring	12	Lotus	91	Ford Cosworth	V8	engine	12	r
29/08	SWITZERLAND	Dijon Prenois	12	Lotus	91	Ford Cosworth	V8		26	8
12/09	ITALY	Monza	12	Lotus	91	Ford Cosworth	V8		23	7
25/09	USA CAESARS PALACE	Las Vegas	12	Lotus	91	Ford Cosworth	V8	accident	21	r

1983

Date	Country/event	Circuit	Race no.	Car	Model	Engine	Configuration	Notes	Grid position	Result
13/03	BRAZIL	Rio de Janeiro	12	Lotus	92	Ford Cosworth	V8		22	12
27/03	USA West	Long Beach	12	Lotus	92	Ford Cosworth	V8		13	12
10/04	Race of Champions	Brands Hatch	12	Lotus	93T	Renault	V6t	handling	8	r
17/04	FRANCE	Paul Ricard	12	Lotus	92	Ford Cosworth	V8	driver discomfort	18	r
01/05	SAN MARINO	Imola	12	Lotus	92	Ford Cosworth	V8	rear wing/accident	15	12r
15/05	MONACO	Monte Carlo	12	Lotus	92	Ford Cosworth	V8	accident	14	r
22/05	BELGIUM	Spa Francorchamps	12	Lotus	92	Ford Cosworth	V8	gearbox	19	r

Date	Country/event	Circuit	Race no.	Car	Model	Engine	Configuration	Notes	Grid position	Result
05/06	USA	Detroit	12	Lotus	92	Ford Cosworth	V8		14	6
12/06	CANADA	Montréal	12	Lotus	92	Ford Cosworth	V8	handling/tyres	18	r
16/07	BRITAIN	Silverstone	12	Lotus	94T	Renault	V6t			4
			12	Lotus	93T	Renault	V6t	practice only	18	
07/08	GERMANY	Hockenheim	12	Lotus	94T	Renault	V6t	engine		r
			12	Lotus	93T	Renault	V6t	practice only	17	
14/08	AUSTRIA	Österreichring	12	Lotus	94T	Renault	V6t		3	5
28/08	NETHERLANDS	Zandvoort	12	Lotus	94T	Renault	V6t	spin	5	r
11/09	ITALY	Monza	12	Lotus	94T	Renault	V6t		11	8
25/09	EUROPE	Brands Hatch	12	Lotus	94T	Renault	V6t	fastest lap	3	3
15/10	SOUTH AFRICA	Kyalami	12	Lotus	94T	Renault	V6t		7	nc

1984

Date	Country/event	Circuit	Race no.	Car	Model	Engine	Configuration	Notes	Grid position	Result
25/03	BRAZIL	Rio de Janeiro	12	Lotus	95T	Renault	V6t	accident	5	r
07/04	SOUTH AFRICA	Kyalami	12	Lotus	95T	Renault	V6t	turbo inlet duct	3	r
29/04	BELGIUM	Zolder	12	Lotus	95T	Renault	V6t	clutch	10	r
06/05	SAN MARINO	Imola	12	Lotus	95T	Renault	V6t	brakes/spin	18	r
20/05	FRANCE	Dijon Prenois	12	Lotus	95T	Renault	V6t		6	3
03/06	MONACO	Monte Carlo	12	Lotus	95T	Renault	V6t	accident	2	r
17/06	CANADA	Montréal	12	Lotus	95T	Renault	V6t		7	6
24/06	USA	Detroit	12	Lotus	95T	Renault	V6t	gearbox	3	r
08/07	USA	Dallas	12	Lotus	95T	Renault	V6t	gearbox	1	6r
22/07	BRITAIN	Brands Hatch	12	Lotus	95T	Renault	V6t	gearbox	8	r
05/08	GERMANY	Hockenheim	12	Lotus	95T	Renault	V6t		16	4
19/08	AUSTRIA	Österreichring	12	Lotus	95T	Renault	V6t	engine	8	r
26/08	NETHERLANDS	Zandvoort	12	Lotus	95T	Renault	V6t		12	3
09/09	ITALY	Monza	12	Lotus	95T	Renault	V6t	spin	7	r
07/10	EUROPE	Nürburgring	12	Lotus	95T	Renault	V6t	engine	8	r
21/10	PORTUGAL	Estoril	12	Lotus	95T	Renault	V6t	brake fluid loss/spin	6	r

1985

Date	Country/event	Circuit	Race no.	Car	Model	Engine	Configuration	Notes	Grid position	Result
07/04	BRAZIL	Rio de Janeiro	5	Williams	FW10	Honda	V6t	accident/exhaust	5	r
21/04	PORTUGAL	Estoril	5	Williams	FW10	Honda	V6t		9	5
05/05	SAN MARINO	Imola	5	Williams	FW10	Honda	V6t		7	5
19/05	MONACO	Monte Carlo	5	Williams	FW10	Honda	V6t		2	7
16/06	CANADA	Montréal	5	Williams	FW10	Honda	V6t		16	6
23/06	USA	Detroit	5	Williams	FW10	Honda	V6t	brakes/accident	2	r
07/07	FRANCE	Paul Ricard	5	Williams	FW10	Honda	V6t	accident/injury		ns
21/07	BRITAIN	Silverstone	5	Williams	FW10	Honda	V6t	clutch	5	r
04/08	GERMANY	Nürburgring	5	Williams	FW10	Honda	V6t		10	6
18/08	AUSTRIA	Österreichring	5	Williams	FW10	Honda	V6t	oil pressure/engine	2	r
25/08	NETHERLANDS	Zandvoort	5	Williams	FW10	Honda	V6t		7	6
08/09	ITALY	Monza	5	Williams	FW10	Honda	V6t	fastest lap/engine	3	11r
15/09	BELGIUM	Spa Francorchamps	5	Williams	FW10	Honda	V6t		7	2
06/10	EUROPE	Brands Hatch	5	Williams	FW10	Honda	V6t		3	1
19/10	SOUTH AFRICA	Kyalami	5	Williams	FW10	Honda	V6t		1	1
03/11	AUSTRALIA	Adelaide	5	Williams	FW10	Honda	V6t	crown wheel & pinion	2	r

1986

Date	Country/event	Circuit	Race no.	Car	Model	Engine	Configuration	Notes	Grid position	Result
23/03	BRAZIL	Rio de Janeiro	5	Williams	FW11	Honda	V6t	accident	3	r
13/04	SPAIN	Jérez de la Frontera	5	Williams	FW11	Honda	V6t	fastest lap	3	2
27/04	SAN MARINO	Imola	5	Williams	FW11	Honda	V6t	engine	3	r
11/05	MONACO	Monte Carlo	5	Williams	FW11	Honda	V6t		2	4
25/05	BELGIUM	Spa Francorchamps	5	Williams	FW11	Honda	V6t		5	1
15/06	CANADA	Montréal	5	Williams	FW11	Honda	V6t		1	1
22/06	USA	Detroit	5	Williams	FW11	Honda	V6t		2	5
06/07	FRANCE	Paul Ricard	5	Williams	FW11	Honda	V6t	fastest lap	2	1
13/07	BRITAIN	Brands Hatch	5	Williams	FW11	Honda	V6t	fastest lap	2	1
27/07	GERMANY	Hockenheim	5	Williams	FW11	Honda	V6t		6	3
10/08	HUNGARY	Hungaroring	5	Williams	FW11	Honda	V6t		4	3
17/08	AUSTRIA	Österreichring	5	Williams	FW11	Honda	V6t	cv joint	6	r
07/09	ITALY	Monza	5	Williams	FW11	Honda	V6t		3	2
21/09	PORTUGAL	Estoril	5	Williams	FW11	Honda	V6t	fastest lap	2	1
12/10	MEXICO	Mexico City	5	Williams	FW11	Honda	V6t		3	5
26/10	AUSTRALIA	Adelaide	5	Williams	FW11	Honda	V6t	rear tyre burst/accident	1	r

1987

Date	Country/event	Circuit	Race no.	Car	Model	Engine	Configuration	Notes	Grid position	Result
12/04	BRAZIL	Rio de Janeiro	5	Williams	FW11B	Honda	V6t		1	6
03/05	SAN MARINO	Imola	5	Williams	FW11B	Honda	V6t		2	1
17/05	BELGIUM	Spa Francorchamps	5	Williams	FW11B	Honda	V6t	accident/undertray	1	r
31/05	MONACO	Monte Carlo	5	Williams	FW11B	Honda	V6t	turbo wastegate	1	r
21/06	USA	Detroit	5	Williams	FW11B	Honda	V6t		1	5
05/07	FRANCE	Paul Ricard	5	Williams	FW11B	Honda	V6t		1	1
12/07	BRITAIN	Silverstone	5	Williams	FW11B	Honda	V6t	fastest lap	2	1
26/07	GERMANY	Hockenheim	5	Williams	FW11B	Honda	V6t	fastest lap/engine	1	r
09/08	HUNGARY	Hungaroring	5	Williams	FW11B	Honda	V6t	rear wheel nut lost	1	14r
16/08	AUSTRIA	Österreichring	5	Williams	FW11B	Honda	V6t	fastest lap	2	1
06/09	ITALY	Monza	5	Williams	FW11B	Honda	V6t		2	3
20/09	PORTUGAL	Estoril	5	Williams	FW11B	Honda	V6t	electrics	2	r
27/09	SPAIN	Jérez de la Frontera	5	Williams	FW11B	Honda	V6t		2	1
18/10	MEXICO	Mexico City	5	Williams	FW11B	Honda	V6t		1	1
01/11	JAPAN	Suzuka	5	Williams	FW11B	Honda	V6t	accident/injury	-	ns

1988

Date	Country/event	Circuit	Race no.	Car	Model	Engine	Configuration	Notes	Grid position	Result
03/04	BRAZIL	Rio de Janeiro	5	Williams	FW12	Judd	V8	electrics/engine	2	r
01/05	SAN MARINO	Imola	5	Williams	FW12	Judd	V8	electrics	11	r
15/05	MONACO	Monte Carlo	5	Williams	FW12	Judd	V8	accident	5	r
29/05	MEXICO	Mexico City	5	Williams	FW12	Judd	V8	engine	14	r
12/06	CANADA	Montréal	5	Williams	FW12	Judd	V8	engine	9	r
19/06	USA	Detroit	5	Williams	FW12	Judd	V8	electrics	6	r
03/07	FRANCE	Paul Ricard	5	Williams	FW12	Judd	V8	front suspension	9	r
10/07	BRITAIN	Silverstone	5	Williams	FW12	Judd	V8	fastest lap	11	2
24/07	GERMANY	Hockenheim	5	Williams	FW12	Judd	V8	accident	11	r
07/08	HUNGARY	Hungaroring	5	Williams	FW12	Judd	V8	driver exhausted	2	r
25/09	PORTUGAL	Estoril	5	Williams	FW12	Judd	V8	accident	6	r
02/10	SPAIN	Jérez de la Frontera	5	Williams	FW12	Judd	V8		3	2
30/10	JAPAN	Suzuka	5	Williams	FW12	Judd	V8	accident	8	r
13/11	AUSTRALIA	Adelaide	5	Williams	FW12	Judd	V8	brakes/accident	3	r

1989

Date	Country/event	Circuit	Race no.	Car	Model	Engine	Configuration	Notes	Grid position	Result
26/03	BRAZIL	Rio de Janeiro	27	Ferrari	640	Ferrari	V12		6	1
23/04	SAN MARINO	Imola	27	Ferrari	640	Ferrari	V12	gearbox	3	r
07/05	MONACO	Monte Carlo	27	Ferrari	640	Ferrari	V12	gearbox	5	r
28/05	MEXICO	Mexico City	27	Ferrari	640	Ferrari	V12	fastest lap/hydraulics	3	r
04/06	USA	Phoenix	27	Ferrari	640	Ferrari	V12	gearbox	4	r
18/06	CANADA	Montréal	27	Ferrari	640	Ferrari	V12	started from pits too soon	5	dq
09/07	FRANCE	Paul Ricard	27	Ferrari	640	Ferrari	V12		3	2
16/07	BRITAIN	Silverstone	27	Ferrari	640	Ferrari	V12	fastest lap	3	2
30/07	GERMANY	Hockenheim	27	Ferrari	640	Ferrari	V12		3	3
13/08	HUNGARY	Hungaroring	27	Ferrari	640	Ferrari	V12	fastest lap	12	1
27/08	BELGIUM	Spa Francorchamps	27	Ferrari	640	Ferrari	V12		6	3
10/09	ITALY	Monza	27	Ferrari	640	Ferrari	V12	gearbox	3	r
24/09	PORTUGAL	Estoril	27	Ferrari	640	Ferrari	V12	accident (disqualified)	3	r/dq
22/10	JAPAN	Suzuka	27	Ferrari	640	Ferrari	V12	engine	4	r
05/11	AUSTRALIA	Adelaide	27	Ferrari	640	Ferrari	V12	accident	7	r

1990

Date	Country/event	Circuit	Race no.	Car	Model	Engine	Configuration	Notes	Grid position	Result
11/03	USA	Phoenix	2	Ferrari	641	Ferrari	V12	engine/clutch/spin/fire	17	r
25/03	BRAZIL	Interlagos	2	Ferrari	641	Ferrari	V12		5	4
13/05	SAN MARINO	Imola	2	Ferrari	641/2	Ferrari	V12	engine	5	r
27/05	MONACO	Monte Carlo	2	Ferrari	641/2	Ferrari	V12	battery/gearbox	7	r
10/06	CANADA	Montréal	2	Ferrari	641/2	Ferrari	V12		7	3
24/06	MEXICO	Mexico City	2	Ferrari	641/2	Ferrari	V12		4	2
08/07	FRANCE	Paul Ricard	2	Ferrari	641/2	Ferrari	V12	fastest lap/engine	1	18r
15/07	BRITAIN	Silverstone	2	Ferrari	641/2	Ferrari	V12	fastest lap/gearbox	1	r
29/07	GERMANY	Hockenheim	2	Ferrari	641/2	Ferrari	V12	undertray damage	4	r
12/08	HUNGARY	Hungaroring	2	Ferrari	641/2	Ferrari	V12	accident	5	17r
26/08	BELGIUM	Spa Francorchamps	2	Ferrari	641/2	Ferrari	V12	handling	5	r
09/09	ITALY	Monza	2	Ferrari	641/2	Ferrari	V12		4	4
23/09	PORTUGAL	Estoril	2	Ferrari	641/2	Ferrari	V12		1	1
30/09	SPAIN	Jérez de la Frontera	2	Ferrari	641/2	Ferrari	V12		3	2
21/10	JAPAN	Suzuka	2	Ferrari	641/2	Ferrari	V12	driveshaft	3	r
04/11	AUSTRALIA	Adelaide	2	Ferrari	641/2	Ferrari	V12	fastest lap	3	2

1991

Date	Country/event	Circuit	Race no.	Car	Model	Engine	Configuration	Notes	Grid position	Result
10/03	USA	Phoenix	5	Williams	FW14	Renault	V10	gearbox	4	r
24/03	BRAZIL	Interlagos	5	Williams	FW14	Renault	V10	fastest lap/gearbox	3	r
28/04	SAN MARINO	Imola	5	Williams	FW14	Renault	V10	accident	4	r
12/05	MONACO	Monte Carlo	5	Williams	FW14	Renault	V10		5	2
02/06	CANADA	Montréal	5	Williams	FW14	Renault	V10	fastest lap/gearbox	2	6r
16/06	MEXICO	Mexico City	5	Williams	FW14	Renault	V10	fastest lap	2	2
07/07	FRANCE	Magny Cours	5	Williams	FW14	Renault	V10	fastest lap	4	1
14/07	BRITAIN	Silverstone	5	Williams	FW14	Renault	V10	fastest lap	1	1
28/07	GERMANY	Hockenheim	5	Williams	FW14	Renault	V10		1	1
11/08	HUNGARY	Hungaroring	5	Williams	FW14	Renault	V10		3	2
25/08	BELGIUM	Spa Francorchamps	5	Williams	FW14	Renault	V10	voltage regulator	3	r
08/09	ITALY	Monza	5	Williams	FW14	Renault	V10		2	1
22/09	PORTUGAL	Estoril	5	Williams	FW14	Renault	V10	fastest lap/accident	4	dq
29/09	SPAIN	Montmeló	5	Williams	FW14	Renault	V10		2	1
20/10	JAPAN	Suzuka	5	Williams	FW14	Renault	V10	brakes/spin	3	r
03/11	AUSTRALIA	Adelaide	5	Williams	FW14	Renault	V10		3	2

1992

Date	Country/event	Circuit	Race no.	Car	Model	Engine	Configuration	Notes	Grid position	Result
01/03	SOUTH AFRICA	Kyalami	5	Williams	FW14B	Renault	V10	fastest lap	1	1
22/03	MEXICO	Mexico City	5	Williams	FW14B	Renault	V10		1	1
05/04	BRAZIL	Interlagos	5	Williams	FW14B	Renault	V10		1	1
03/05	SPAIN	Montmeló	5	Williams	FW14B	Renault	V10	fastest lap	1	1
17/05	SAN MARINO	Imola	5	Williams	FW14B	Renault	V10		1	1
31/05	MONACO	Monte Carlo	5	Williams	FW14B	Renault	V10	fastest lap	1	2
14/06	CANADA	Montréal	5	Williams	FW14B	Renault	V10	accident	3	r
05/07	FRANCE	Magny Cours	5	Williams	FW14B	Renault	V10	fastest lap	1	1
12/07	BRITAIN	Silverstone	5	Williams	FW14B	Renault	V10	fastest lap	1	1

Date	Country/event	Circuit	Race no.	Car	Model	Engine	Configuration	Notes	Grid position	Result
26/07	GERMANY	Hockenheim	5	Williams	FW14B	Renault	V10		1	1
16/08	HUNGARY	Hungaroring	5	Williams	FW14B	Renault	V10	fastest lap	2	2
30/08	BELGIUM	Spa Francorchamps	5	Williams	FW14B	Renault	V10		1	2
13/09	ITALY	Monza	5	Williams	FW14B	Renault	V10	fastest lap/hydraulics	1	r
27/09	PORTUGAL	Estoril	5	Williams	FW14B	Renault	V10		1	1
25/10	JAPAN	Suzuka	5	Williams	FW14B	Renault	V10	fastest lap/engine	1	r
08/11	AUSTRALIA	Adelaide	5	Williams	FW14B	Renault	V10	accident	1	r

1993

Date	Country/event	Circuit	Race no.	Car	Model	Engine	Configuration	Notes	Grid position	Result
21/03	PPG IndyCar World Series	Surfers Paradise	5	Lola	L93/00	Ford Cosworth	V8		1	1
04/04	PPG IndyCar World Series	Phoenix	5	Lola	L93/00	Ford Cosworth	V8	accident in practice		ns
18/04	PPG IndyCar World Series	Long Beach	5	Lola	L93/00	Ford Cosworth	V8		1	3
30/05	PPG IndyCar World Series	Indianapolis 500	5	Lola	L93/00	Ford Cosworth	V8		8	3
06/06	PPG IndyCar World Series	Milwaukee	5	Lola	L93/00	Ford Cosworth	V8		7	1
13/06	PPG IndyCar World Series	Detroit	5	Lola	L93/00	Ford Cosworth	V8		1	15
27/06	PPG IndyCar World Series	Portland	5	Lola	L93/00	Ford Cosworth	V8		1	2
11/07	PPG IndyCar World Series	Cleveland	5	Lola	L93/00	Ford Cosworth	V8		2	3
18/07	PPG IndyCar World Series	Toronto	5	Lola	L93/00	Ford Cosworth	V8	wastegate	9	r
01/08	PPG IndyCar World Series	Michigan	5	Lola	L93/00	Ford Cosworth	V8		2	1
08/08	PPG IndyCar World Series	New Hampshire	5	Lola	L93/00	Ford Cosworth	V8		1	1
22/08	PPG IndyCar World Series	Elkhart Lake	5	Lola	L93/00	Ford Cosworth	V8		2	2
29/08	PPG IndyCar World Series	Vancouver	5	Lola	L93/00	Ford Cosworth	V8		3	6
12/09	PPG IndyCar World Series	Mid-Ohio	5	Lola	L93/00	Ford Cosworth	V8		1	12
19/09	PPG IndyCar World Series	Nazareth	5	Lola	L93/00	Ford Cosworth	V8		1	1
03/10	PPG IndyCar World Series	Laguna Seca	5	Lola	L93/00	Ford Cosworth	V8	accident	3	r
31/10	TOCA Shootout	Donington Park	5	Ford	Mondeo	Ford	V6	accident	13	r

1994

Date	Country/event	Circuit	Race no.	Car	Model	Engine	Configuration	Notes	Grid position	Result
20/03	PPG IndyCar World Series	Surfers Paradise	5	Lola	L94/00	Ford Cosworth	V8		1	9
10/04	PPG IndyCar World Series	Phoenix	5	Lola	L94/00	Ford Cosworth	V8		3	3
17/04	PPG IndyCar World Series	Long Beach	5	Lola	L94/00	Ford Cosworth	V8		4	2
29/05	PPG IndyCar World Series	Indianapolis 500	5	Lola	L94/00	Ford Cosworth	V8	accident	7	r
05/06	PPG IndyCar World Series	Milwaukee	5	Lola	L94/00	Ford Cosworth	V8		9	5
12/06	PPG IndyCar World Series	Detroit	5	Lola	L94/00	Ford Cosworth	V8	engine	1	r
26/06	PPG IndyCar World Series	Portland	5	Lola	L94/00	Ford Cosworth	V8		2	5
03/07	FRANCE	Magny Cours	2	Williams	FW16	Renault	V10	transmission	2	r
10/07	PPG IndyCar World Series	Cleveland	5	Lola	L94/00	Ford Cosworth	V8		4	2
17/07	PPG IndyCar World Series	Toronto	5	Lola	L94/00	Ford Cosworth	V8	handling	2	r
31/07	PPG IndyCar World Series	Michigan	5	Lola	L94/00	Ford Cosworth	V8	throttle linkage	1	r
14/08	PPG IndyCar World Series	Mid-Ohio	5	Lola	L94/00	Ford Cosworth	V8		4	7
21/08	PPG IndyCar World Series	New Hampshire	5	Lola	L94/00	Ford Cosworth	V8	accident/ suspension	3	r
04/09	PPG IndyCar World Series	Vancouver	5	Lola	L94/00	Ford Cosworth	V8		2	10
11/09	PPG IndyCar World Series	Elkhart Lake	5	Lola	L94/00	Ford Cosworth	V8		3	13
18/09	PPG IndyCar World Series	Nazareth	5	Lola	L94/00	Ford Cosworth	V8	handling	3	r
10/10	PPG IndyCar World Series	Laguna Seca	5	Lola	L94/00	Ford Cosworth	V8		3	8
16/10	EUROPE	Jérez de la Frontera	2	Williams	FW16B	Renault	V10	spin	3	r
06/11	JAPAN	Suzuka	2	Williams	FW16B	Renault	V10		4	4
13/11	AUSTRALIA	Adelaide	2	Williams	FW16B	Renault	V10		1	1

1995

Date	Country/event	Circuit	Race no.	Car	Model	Engine	Configuration	Notes	Grid position	Result
30/04	SAN MARINO	Imola	7	McLaren	MP4/1	Mercedes-Benz	V10		9	10
14/05	SPAIN	Montmeló	7	McLaren	MP4/1	Mercedes-Benz	V10	handling	10	r

1998

Date	Country/event	Circuit	Race no.	Car	Model	Engine	Configuration	Notes	Grid position	Result
14/06	BTCC	Donington Park	55	Ford	Mondeo	Ford	V6	accident	3	r
			55	Ford	Mondeo	Ford	V6		19	5
31/08	BTCC	Brands Hatch	55	Ford	Mondeo	Ford	V6	accident	18	r
			55	Ford	Mondeo	Ford	V6	accident	20	r
20/09	BTCC	Silverstone	55	Ford	Mondeo	Ford	V6		16	14
			55	Ford	Mondeo	Ford	V6		18	11

2005

Date	Country/event	Circuit	Race no.	Car	Model	Engine	Configuration	Notes	Grid position	Result
13/11	GP Masters	Kyalami	5	Delta	GPM	Ford Cosworth	V8	fastest lap	1	1

2006

Date	Country/event	Circuit	Race no.	Car	Model	Engine	Configuration	Notes	Grid position	Result
29/04	GP Masters	Losail, Qatar	5	Delta	GPM	Ford Cosworth	V8		1	1
13/08	GP Masters	Silverstone	5	Delta	GPM	Ford Cosworth	V8	differential	13	r

2007

Date	Country/event	Circuit	Race no.	Car	Model	Engine	Configuration	Notes	Grid position	Result
06/05	FIA GT	Silverstone	63	Ferrari	430 GT2	Ferrari	V8	with Chris Niarchos	25	21